A NOTE TO THE TEACHER ...

In producing this book we have tried very hard to achieve certain aims ...

1. **To produce excellent revision notes for the end of Key Stage 3 National Curriculum tests ('S.A.T.'s) for levels 3-7 inclusive,** and to ensure that everything in the Programme of Study for this Key Stage is covered - AND NOTHING MORE. Because of the ambiguous nature of the Programme of study, many teachers are unaware of just how much content is actually Key Stage 4 and therefore non-examinable.

2. **To encourage and retain the interest of the younger pupil at Key Stage 3.** In order to do this we have opted for colour, even though we consider black and white a more efficient learning medium for older, Key Stage 4 G.C.S.E. pupils. Nevertheless we have retained the S.R.G. principles of clear concise content presented in an informal user-friendly style.

3. **To cover the material without reference to specific levels.** Every page is accessible to all pupils but clearly some will absorb and understand more than others. All pupils should be encouraged to cover as much as possible of every topic.

4. **To help teachers to make their way through the minefield of the National Curriculum and to provide good homework and realistic test material.** To this end, each page has questions suitable for homework and at the end of each section is a set of 'S.A.T.'s style questions to test learning.

   We feel sure this guide will lighten your load and lead to a significant overall improvement in your National Curriculum Key Stage 3 test results.

A NOTE TO THE PUPIL ...

We're sure that you will enjoy using this book, but to make the most of it, ...

- Don't just read - LEARN ACTIVELY by constantly testing yourself without looking at the book. Try to write down a sequence or label a diagram.

- When you have revised a sub-section or a diagram, place a tick against it, and after revising a page fill in the PROGRESS AND REVISION CHART at the back of the book.

- Jot down anything which will help <u>you</u> to remember.

Good Luck!!

Katie Whelan

CONTENTS

Life Processes and Living Things

Materials and their Properties

Materials and their Properties

Physical Processes

THE 7 LIFE PROCESSES

These processes to some extent are common to all life forms ...

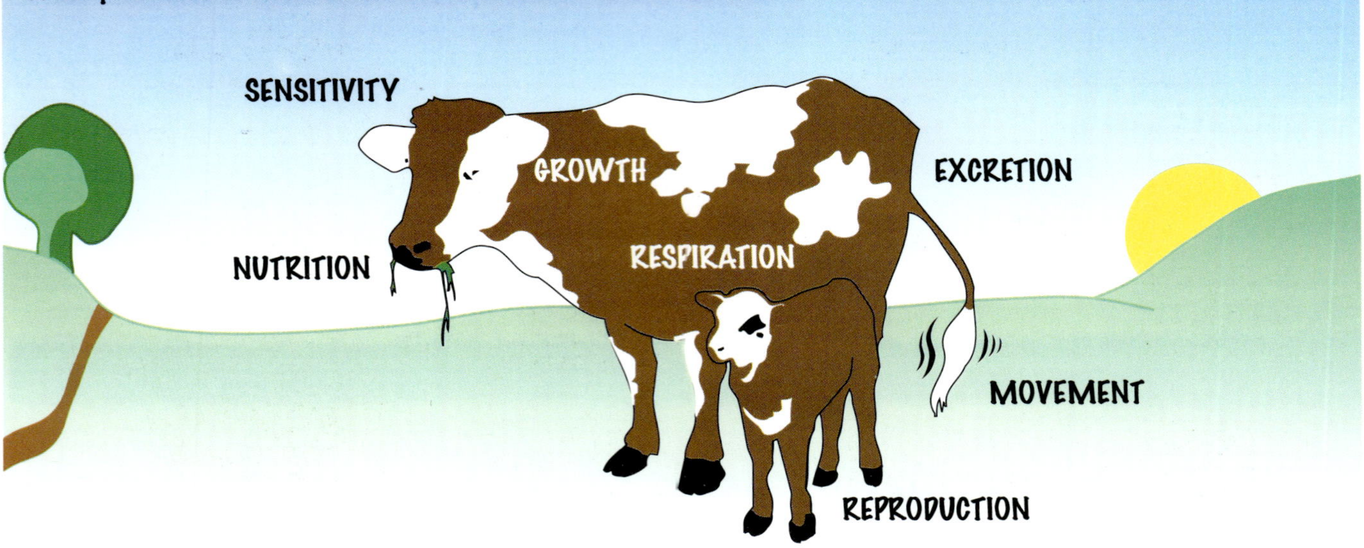

MOVEMENT	Muscles contract and parts of the body move.
REPRODUCTION	All living things need to make 'copies' of themselves.
SENSITIVITY	The ability to respond to change in the surroundings.
GROWTH	Organisms which are born small need to grow into adult size.
RESPIRATION	Oxygen is combined with food to release energy in cells.
EXCRETION	Waste products from reactions in cells must be removed.
NUTRITION	Food is needed for new body structure and energy.

The initial letters of the 7 processes spell **MRS.GREN!** Remember this!
Also remember that plants do all these things ... but less obviously!

CELLS, TISSUES AND ORGANS

A group of cells with similar structure and function is called a **TISSUE**, e.g. MUSCLE TISSUE, NERVOUS TISSUE, BLOOD.

Two or more tissues working together is called an **ORGAN**, e.g. BRAIN, KIDNEY, HEART, LUNG.

As you go through this guide you will see how various organs function to enable the 7 LIFE PROCESSES to take place.

1. Choose an animal and describe how it performs the 7 life processes.
2. Choose a plant and describe how it performs the 7 life processes.

TYPICAL PLANT AND ANIMAL CELLS

All animals and plants are made up of cells ...

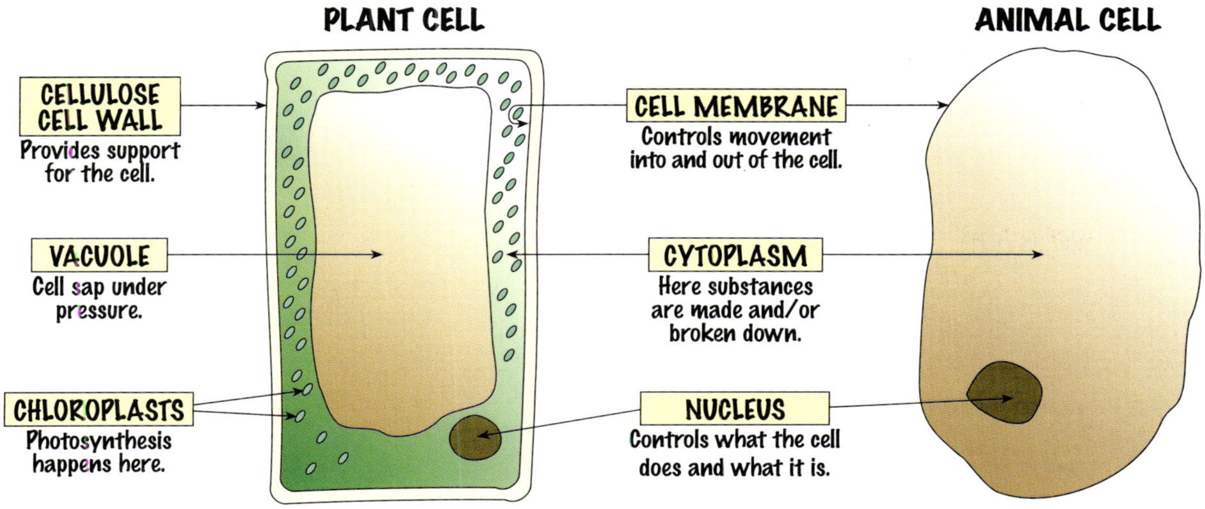

DIFFERENCES BETWEEN ANIMAL AND PLANT CELLS

PLANT CELL	ANIMAL CELL
• Has a CELLULOSE CELL WALL • Has a large central VACUOLE. • Has CHLOROPLASTS in cells which are exposed to light.	• No cellulose cell wall. • If vacuoles present, they are small. • No chloroplasts.

SPECIALISED CELLS

Many cells are highly specialised to do a certain job. We say they are 'ADAPTED TO THEIR FUNCTION.'

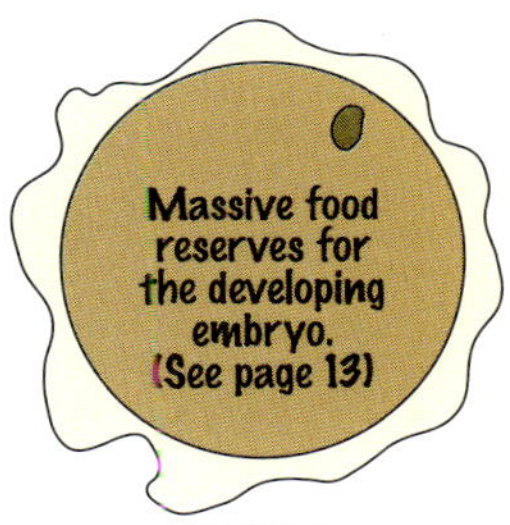

OVUM
(egg cell)

Tiny short lived cell which is amazingly mobile because of its tail. (See page 13)

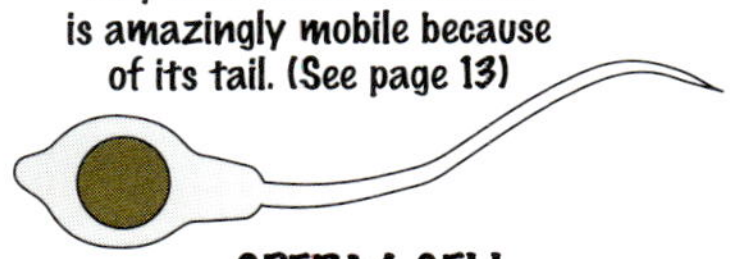

SPERM CELL
(not to same scale as ovum)

5 SPECIALISED CELLS

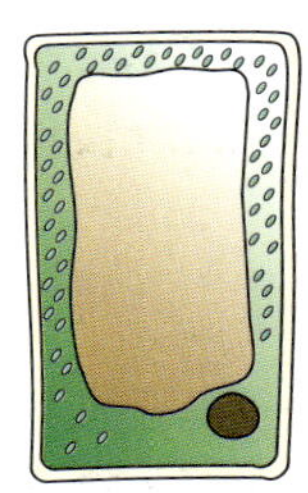

Column - shaped cell on upper surface of leaves - packed with chloroplasts. (See page 16)

PALISADE CELL

These cells produce mucus and the cilia waft it towards the mouth and nose. (See page 9)

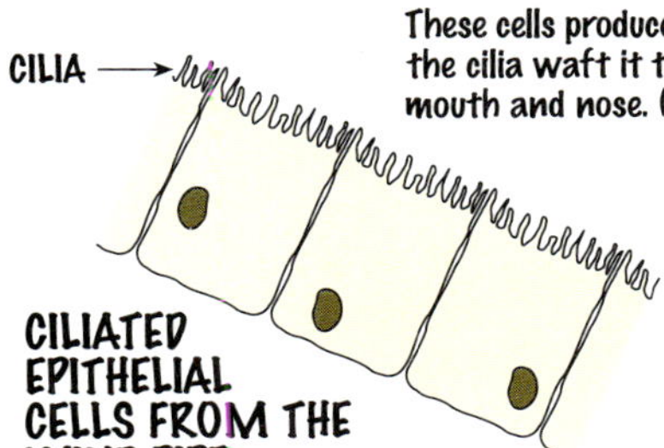

CILIATED EPITHELIAL CELLS FROM THE WIND PIPE.

Thin hair - like projections give a big surface area for efficient absorption. (See page 16)

ROOT HAIR CELL

1. Draw LARGE diagrams of typical plant and animal cells and label them.
Make sure you know these cell features.
2. Draw a table matching the specialised cells above to their 'ADAPTATIONS'.

CONSTITUENTS OF FOOD

A BALANCED DIET

A balanced diet should contain all of the seven food types mentioned below. It's not just a question of eating enough food to stay healthy, you have to eat a variety in order to get the right "balance of essential nutrients," for activity and growth. This means different diets for different people e.g. HIGH PROTEIN for BODY BUILDERS, HIGH CARBOHYDRATES for MANUAL WORKERS, and HIGH PROTEIN, and MINERALS for PREGNANT WOMEN.

THE SEVEN CONSTITUENTS OF FOOD

WHERE WE GET THEM	WHAT THEY ARE	WHAT WE USE THEM FOR
 MEAT FISH EGGS BEANS	**PROTEINS** 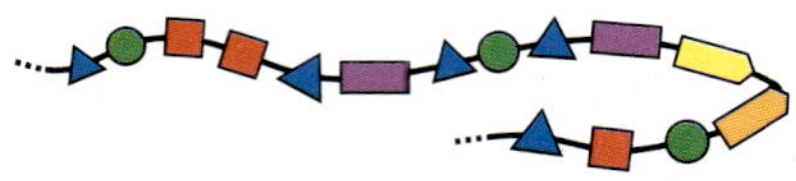 HUGE, LONG CHAINS OF DIFFERENT AMINO ACIDS.	**GROWTH + REPAIR**
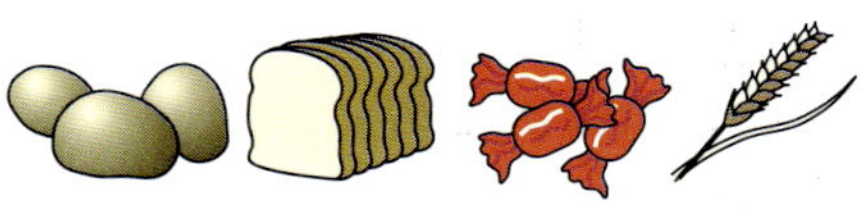 POTATOES BREAD SWEETS CEREALS	**CARBOHYDRATES**  HUGE, LONG CHAINS OF INDENTICAL SUGAR MOLECULES (STARCH) OR,  INDIVIDUAL SUGAR MOLECULES (GLUCOSE).	**ENERGY** THROUGH RESPIRATION.
 MILK BUTTER CHEESE MEAT	**FATS**  INDIVIDUAL FAT MOLECULES.	**STORED ENERGY** AND HEAT INSULATION.
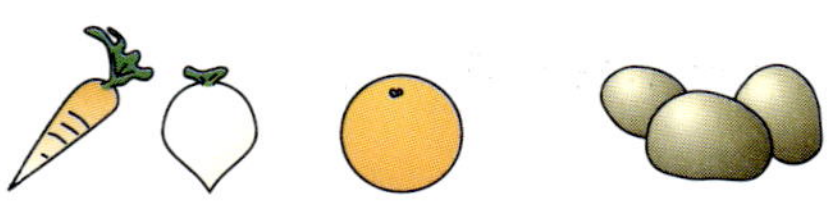 FRESH VEG CITRUS FRUITS UNPROCESSED FOODS	**VITAMINS** ONLY TINY AMOUNTS NEEDED.	**CELL CHEMISTRY** TO KEEP EVERYTHING WORKING O.K.
IRON from  LIVER; CALCIUM from 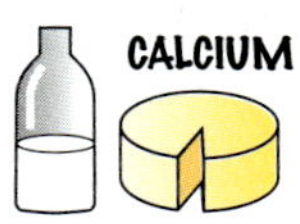 MILK + CHEESE	**MINERALS** IRON and CALCIUM are the ones you need to know.	**IRON – HEALTHY BLOOD** **CALCIUM – BONES and TEETH**
 VEGETABLES FRUIT BREAD	**FIBRE** This is the indigestible part of food.	**PREVENTS CONSTIPATION and BOWEL CANCER**
 ALL KINDS OF DRINKS ... AND NEARLY ALL KINDS OF FOOD	**WATER** Our cells are mainly made up of water.	**TO REPLACE WATER WHICH IS LOST (sweating, urine etc.)**

1. Design a poster illustrating the necessity for a BALANCED DIET. Aim your poster at 11 year olds and make it interesting and eye catching.
2. Look at the nutritional information on as many household food items as you can.

DIGESTING FOOD

DIGESTION

All this means is, THE BREAKING DOWN OF <u>LARGE INSOLUBLE</u> MOLECULES INTO <u>SMALLER SOLUBLE</u> MOLECULES SO THAT THEY CAN BE ABSORBED THROUGH THE WALLS OF THE INTESTINE INTO THE BLOODSTREAM. THIS IS DONE BY SPECIAL PROTEINS CALLED **ENZYMES.**

TEETH

First of all we have to break our food up into smaller pieces, using 4 different types of teeth.

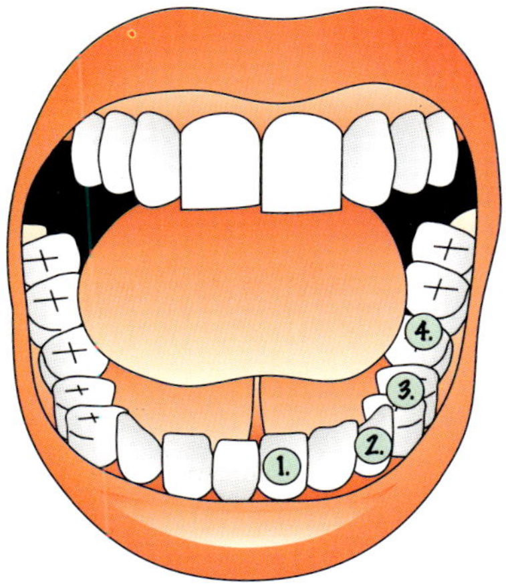

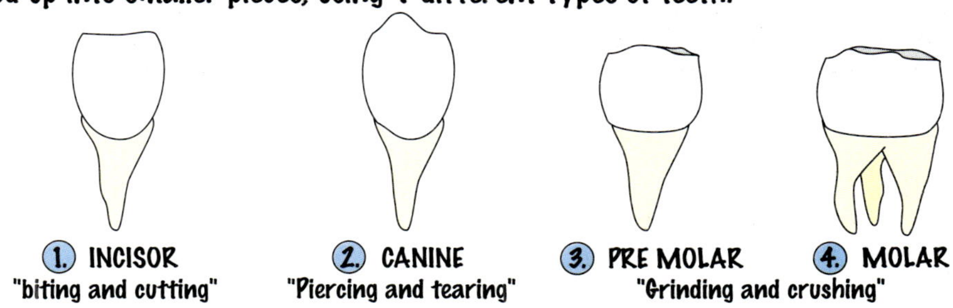

DENTAL CARE

- Sugary food sticks to the teeth ...
- ... allowing BACTERIA to grow, causing PLAQUE.
- Bacteria make ACID which eats away the tooth ...
- ... and eventually gives you TOOTHACHE.

FOR YOUR OWN SAKE, BRUSH YOUR TEETH REGULARLY.

THE DIGESTIVE SYSTEM

Special chemicals called ENZYMES are poured onto the food as it passes through the digestive system, in order to break it down.

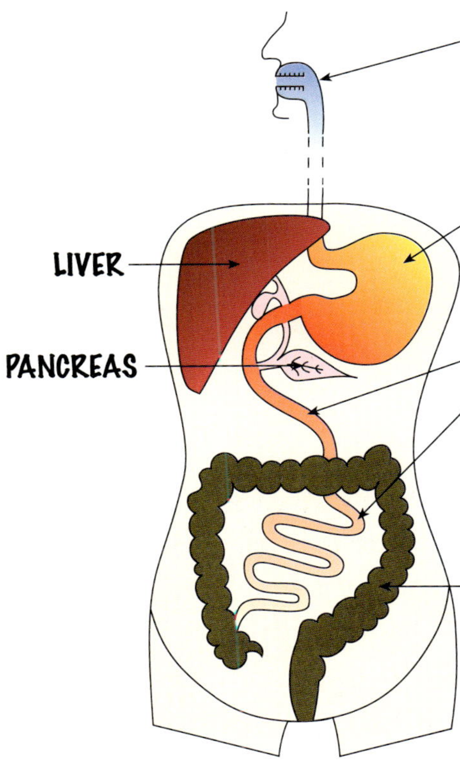

MOUTH

- The food is chewed up and mixed with saliva ...
- ... which contains an ENZYME which breaks down STARCH.

STOMACH

- This is a muscular bag which contains acid to kill bacteria ...
- ... and an ENZYME which breaks down PROTEIN.

SMALL INTESTINE

- The PANCREAS pours more ENZYMES into the small intestine which ...
- ... also provides its own enzymes to ...
- ... break down all the food into SMALL SOLUBLE MOLECULES.
- <u>ALL THE PRODUCTS OF DIGESTION ARE ABSORBED HERE!</u>

LARGE INTESTINE

- By the time the remains of the food get here ...
- ... they are very WET and SLOPPY.
- The large intestine REABSORBS ALL THE WATER from this mess ...
- ... leaving fairly dry INDIGESTIBLE FAECES to be EGESTED (released) from the body.

1. Imagine you swallowed a 1p coin. Describe the journey it would make, and the events which would happen as it passed through the digestive system.
2. Make sure you can label the main regions of the digestive system.

THE HEART AND CIRCULATION

The heart pumps blood through our circulatory system (arteries, veins and capillaries) so that all the cells of the body can receive FOOD and OXYGEN, and have CARBON DIOXIDE and WASTE removed.

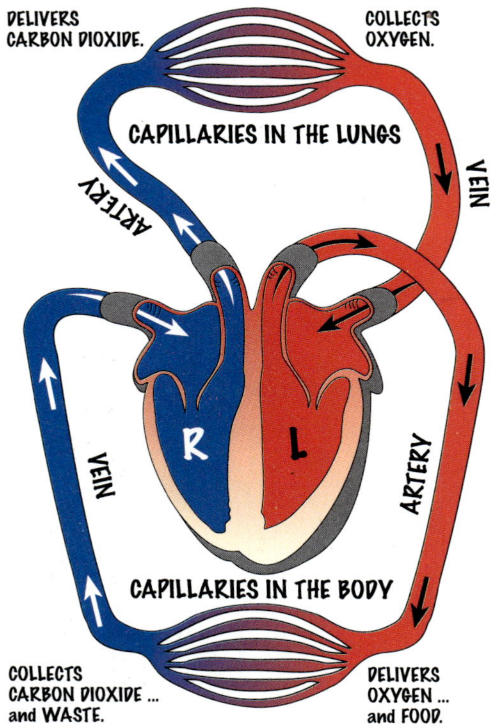

- The heart is made of MUSCLE ...
- ... and pumps the blood in a ...
- ... DOUBLE CIRCULATION ('figure of eight'),
- ... i.e. through the heart TWICE on each circuit.
- Each side acts as a separate pump.
- Arteries carry blood AWAY from the heart.
- Veins carry blood TOWARDS the heart.

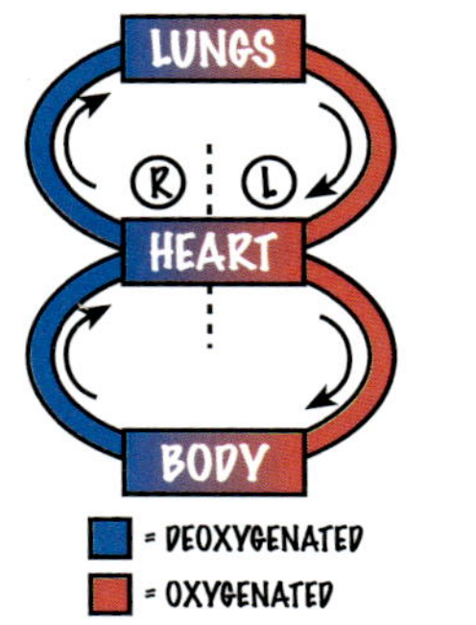

AN EASIER WAY OF LOOKING AT IT ...

- The Right side of the heart pumps ...
- ... DEOXYGENATED blood to the LUNGS ...
- ... to pick up OXYGEN.
- The Left side of the heart pumps this ...
- ... OXYGENATED blood to all parts of the body.

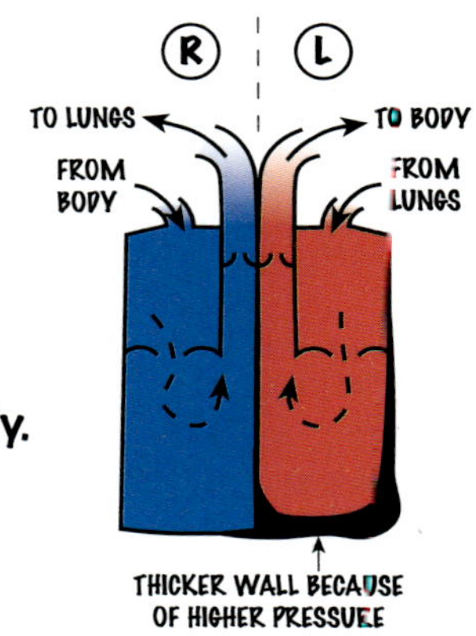

EXCHANGE OF SUBSTANCES AT THE CAPILLARIES

The heart and blood vessels provide a route around the body, but it is the BLOOD which actually TRANSPORTS substances. Exchange of substances between the blood and the body tissues can <u>ONLY</u> OCCUR IN CAPILLARIES.

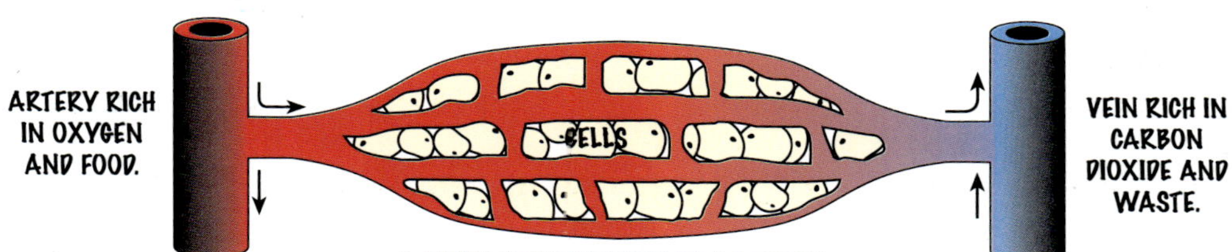

A CAPILLARY NETWORK IN A MUSCLE.

TAKE A CLOSER LOOK!

- OXYGEN is carried by ...
  ... the RED BLOOD CELLS.
- CARBON DIOXIDE, ...
  ... FOOD and WASTE ...
  ... are carried by ...
  ... the PLASMA
  (the watery substance).

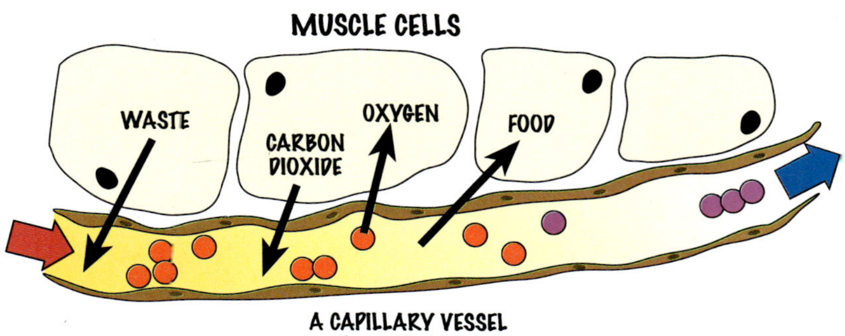

A CAPILLARY VESSEL
(one cell thick)

Write short definitions of CAPILLARIES, ARTERIES, VEINS, RIGHT SIDE OF THE HEART, LEFT SIDE OF THE HEART, DEOXYGENATED BLOOD, OXYGENATED BLOOD.

GAS EXCHANGE

The lungs are our gas-exchange surface where OXYGEN enters the blood and CARBON DIOXIDE leaves it. This table shows how much of the gases are actually swapped ...

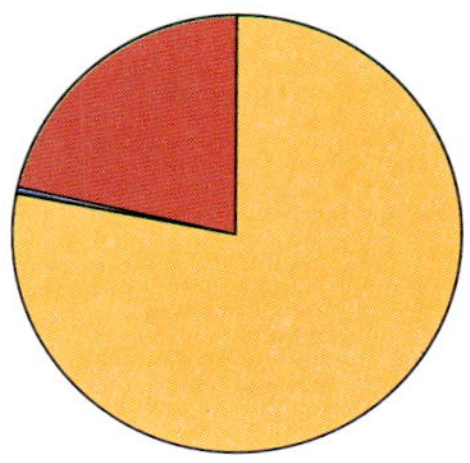

AIR BREATHED IN	%
OXYGEN (nearly)	21
CARBON DIOXIDE	0.03
NITROGEN	79

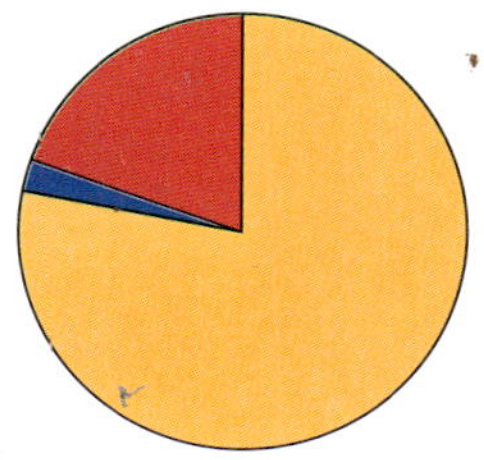

AIR BREATHED OUT	%
OXYGEN (nearly)	18
CARBON DIOXIDE	3
NITROGEN	79

STRUCTURE OF THE LUNGS

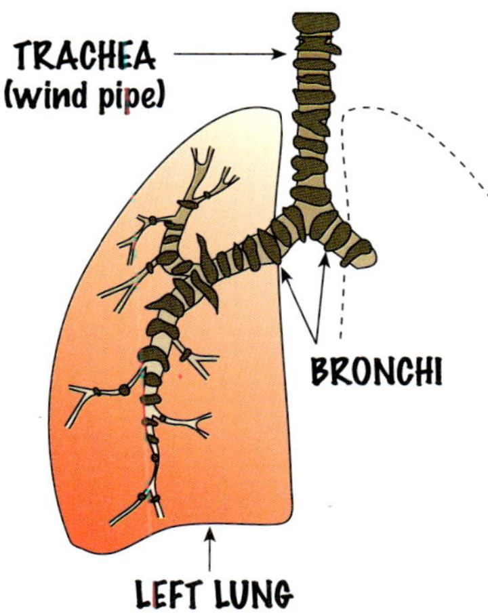

The arrangement of the breathing tubes inside the lungs.

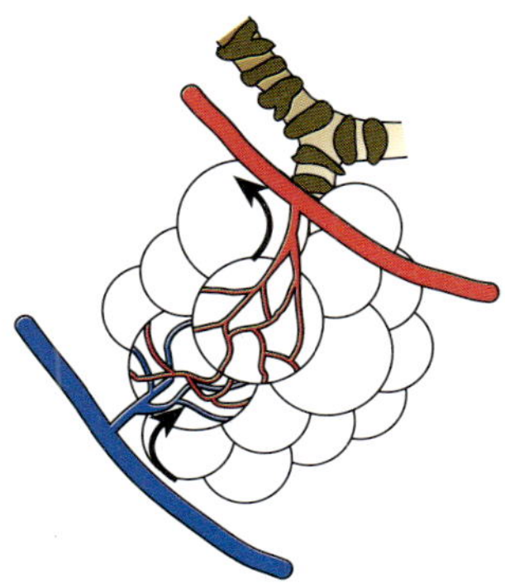

A small group of air sacs and capillaries.

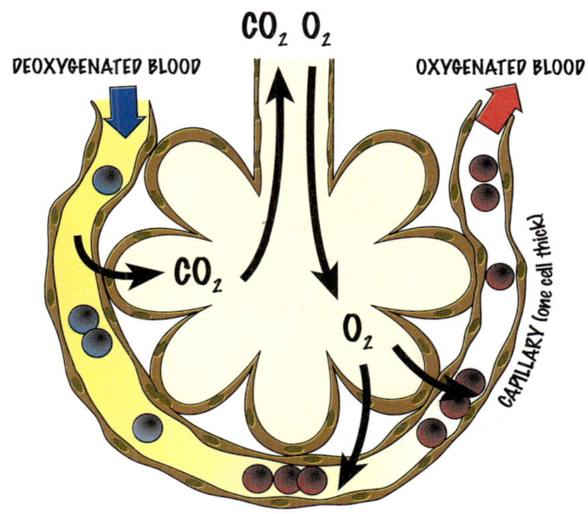

Look how close the capillary vessel is to the air sacs (Both of these are only one cell thick).

- GAS EXCHANGE takes place between the CAPILLARIES and the AIR SACS (Alveoli).
- CARBON DIOXIDE passes out of the BLOOD PLASMA and into the AIR SAC ...
- ... while OXYGEN passes from the AIR SAC into the BLOOD and is picked up by the RED BLOOD CELLS.

The lungs are really well adapted for GAS EXCHANGE because they have ...

1 ... a HUGE SURFACE AREA. 2 ... a MASSIVE BLOOD SUPPLY. 3 ... a MOIST SURFACE. 4 ... VERY THIN WALLS.

THE EFFECTS OF SMOKING

... generally

- CANCER.
- ARTERIAL DISEASE.
- REDUCES O_2 CARRYING CAPACITY.

... on gas exchange

- BRONCHITIS
  Bronchi become narrowed, air sacs are damaged and lungs lose elasticity. Cilia on epithelial cells (See page 5) stop beating mucus up the breathing tubes to the mouth.

... on gas exchange

- EMPHYSEMA
  Continuous coughing damages air sacs, reducing the surface area for gas exchange.

Design a quiz for the rest of the class consisting of 10 well thought out questions on GAS EXCHANGE and the STRUCTURE OF THE LUNGS. Write the questions out fully.

RESPIRATION

FROM THE LUNGS TO THE CELLS ... AND BACK

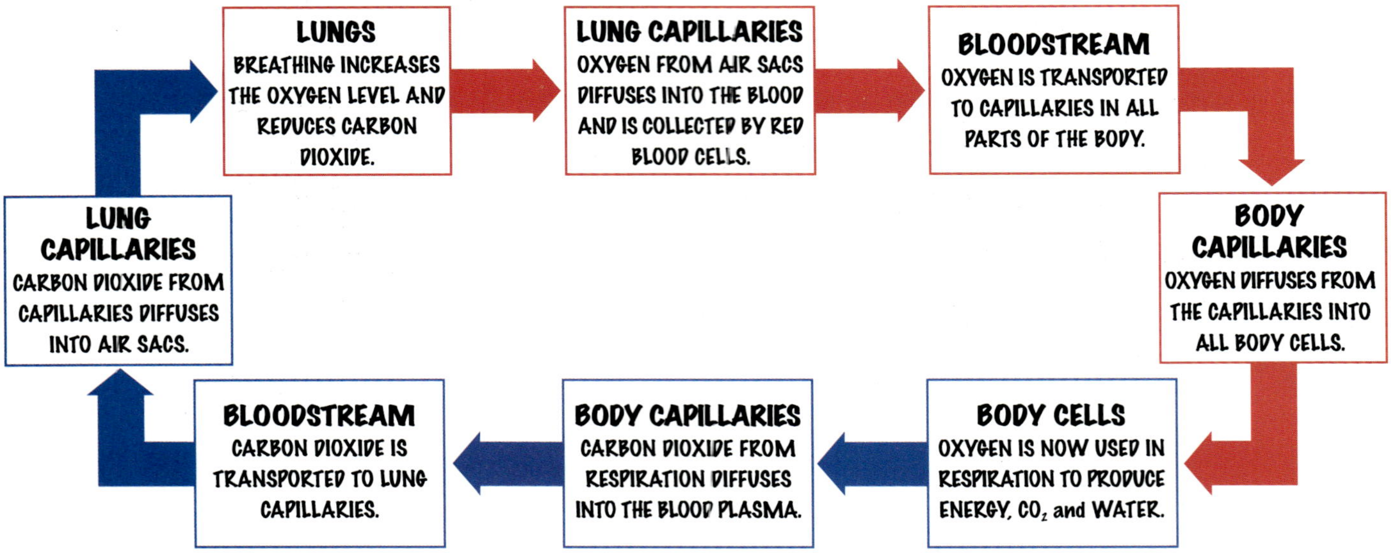

AEROBIC RESPIRATION ...

... is the release of energy from energy-rich molecules by combining them with oxygen inside living cells.

It occurs in both animals and plants.

- The energy-rich molecule is GLUCOSE which is obtained from the digestion of food.
- The oxygen is obtained from breathing.
- Both OXYGEN and GLUCOSE are transported to respiring cells in the bloodstream.
- All cells are close enough to a capillary network to get the oxygen and glucose they need ...
- ... and to get rid of carbon dioxide, water (and other waste products).

Example: A working muscle cell ...

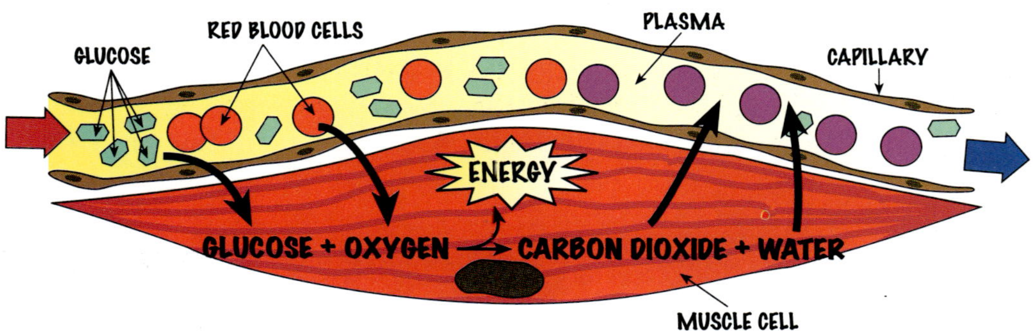

GLUCOSE + OXYGEN ⟶ CARBON DIOXIDE + WATER + ENERGY

This is the equation for RESPIRATION - you must learn this!

THE EFFECT OF EXERCISE

- The harder your muscles work, the more OXYGEN and GLUCOSE they need.
- As these substances are brought to the cells in the blood, the flow of blood must increase.
- For this to happen, the HEART MUST BEAT FASTER, and this is why ...
- ... our PULSE RATE INCREASES WITH EXERCISE.
  (We also breathe more quickly and deeper in order to get more oxygen into the blood.)

1. Write an essay about the journey of a molecule of oxygen from the atmosphere to the cell which 'uses' it.
2. Learn by heart (and I really mean this!) the word equation for AEROBIC RESPIRATION.

BONES, JOINTS AND MUSCLES

THE SKELETON

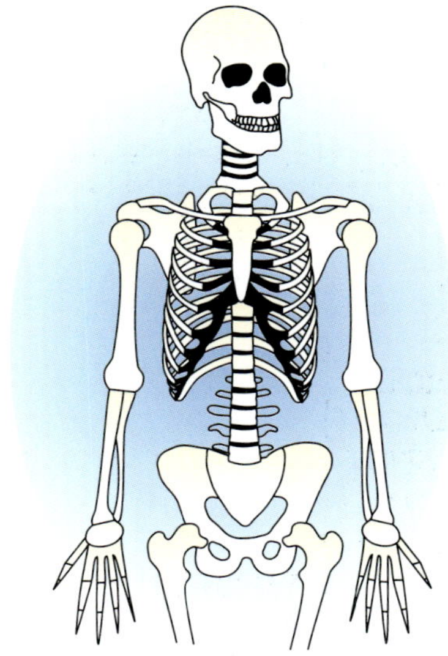

Without a skeleton we would be very floppy.

The Skeleton ...

- ... SUPPORTS OUR SOFT TISSUES ...
- ... PROTECTS VITAL ORGANS (brain, heart and lungs etc.) ...
- ... PROVIDES A FRAMEWORK OF LEVERS FOR MUSCLE ATTACHMENT.

Between the different bones of the skeleton there are JOINTS.

THE JOINTS

- Bones are attached to other bones by <u>SLIGHTLY ELASTIC</u> LIGAMENTS.
- A layer of CARTILAGE prevents wear of the surfaces in contact.
- A small amount of FLUID also helps to reduce friction.

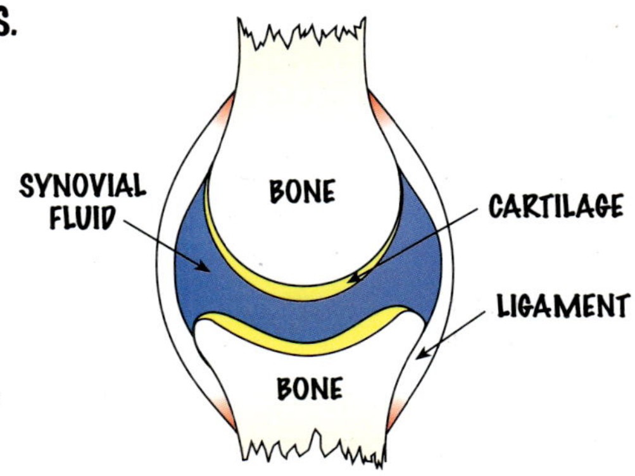

There are several types of joint, the most important of which are ...

1. HINGE JOINTS	Knee joint, Elbow joint.
2. BALL and SOCKET JOINTS	Shoulder joint, Hip joint.
3. PARTLY MOVABLE JOINTS	Joints between Ribs and Breast Bone.
4. FIXED JOINTS	Joints between the Skull bones.

THE MUSCLES

- Muscles can only CONTRACT i.e. shorten, and so can only pull bones.
- Because of this they act in ANTAGONISTIC PAIRS to oppose each other's movement.
- Muscles are attached to bones by <u>NON - ELASTIC</u> TENDONS.

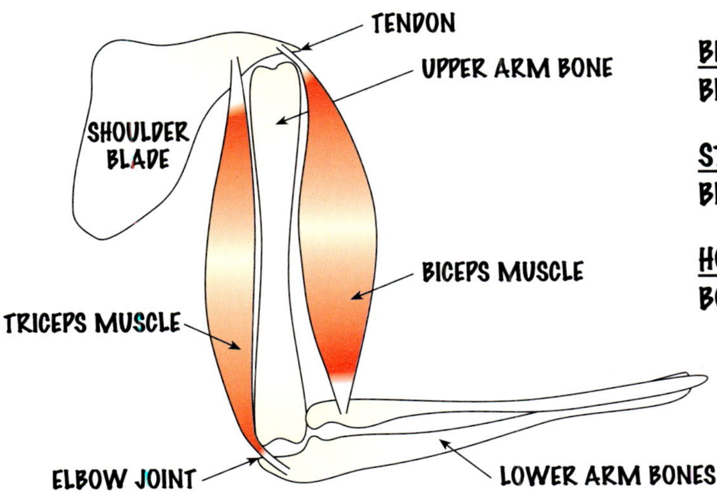

<u>BENDING THE ARM:</u>
BICEPS CONTRACTS and TRICEPS RELAXES.

<u>STRAIGHTENING THE ARM:</u>
BICEPS RELAXES and TRICEPS CONTRACTS.

<u>HOLDING THE ARM RIGID:</u>
BOTH BICEPS and TRICEPS CONTRACT.

1. On the skeleton in the top right hand corner, label as many different types of joint as you can.
2. Draw a ROUGH diagram of a human leg showing how ANTAGONISTIC MUSCLES can work.

ADOLESCENCE

This is the time when a human's reproductive organs become mature, and physically the person changes from a boy or a girl into an adult.

PHYSICAL CHANGES WHICH TAKE PLACE DURING ADOLESCENCE	
GIRLS	**BOYS**
• OVARIES START TO RELEASE EGGS. • BREASTS START TO DEVELOP. • HIPS GET BROADER. • PUBIC AND UNDER ARM HAIR GROWS.	• TESTES START TO PRODUCE SPERM. • MUSCLES AND PENIS GROW BIGGER. • VOICE BECOMES DEEPER. • PUBIC, FACIAL AND UNDERARM HAIR GROWS.

These physical changes are also accompanied by EMOTIONAL CHANGES, caused by changing levels of hormones in the body. These may include ...

• ... interest in the opposite sex, • ... irritability, • ... mood swings, • ... embarrassment.

At this time there is often friction with parents ... but most of us get through it O.K.

FEMALE REPRODUCTIVE SYSTEM

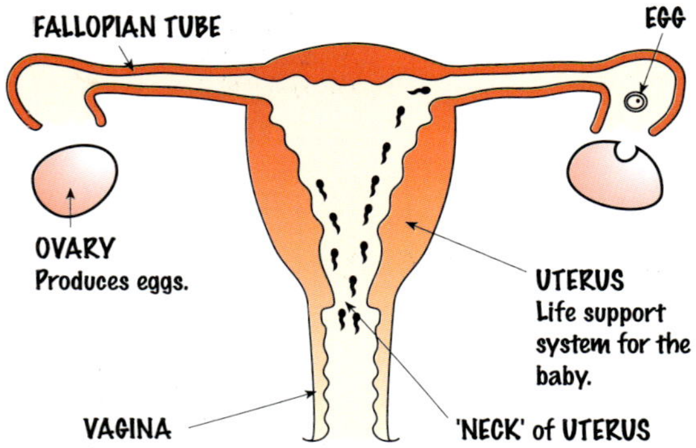

- An egg is released MONTHLY by alternate ovaries ...
- ... and moves into the FALLOPIAN TUBE (oviduct).
- If sexual intercourse has taken place then sperm will swim through the UTERUS ...
- ... and up into the FALLOPIAN TUBES ...
- ... where FERTILISATION may occur if a sperm fuses with the egg.

MALE REPRODUCTIVE SYSTEM

- Sperm is continually produced in the TESTES.
- When sexually aroused the PENIS becomes erect ...
- ... and may be inserted into the VAGINA.
- Sperms are then EJACULATED into the vagina ...
- ... and may eventually fertilise the OVUM (egg).

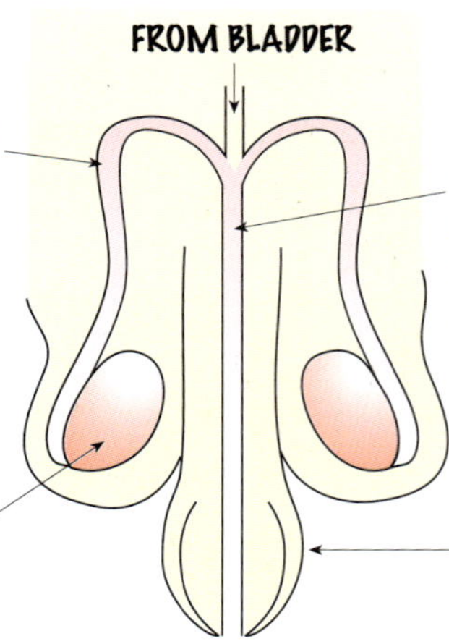

Practice labelling the diagrams of the female and male reproductive systems.

Do this by cutting a hole in a sheet of paper which is just big enough to allow you to see the diagram but not the labels.

THE MENSTRUAL CYCLE

Between the ages of approximately 13 and 50, a woman is fertile and the lining of her uterus is replaced every month. This is a PERIOD. We can represent the changes in the uterus wall which occur over 28 days like this ...

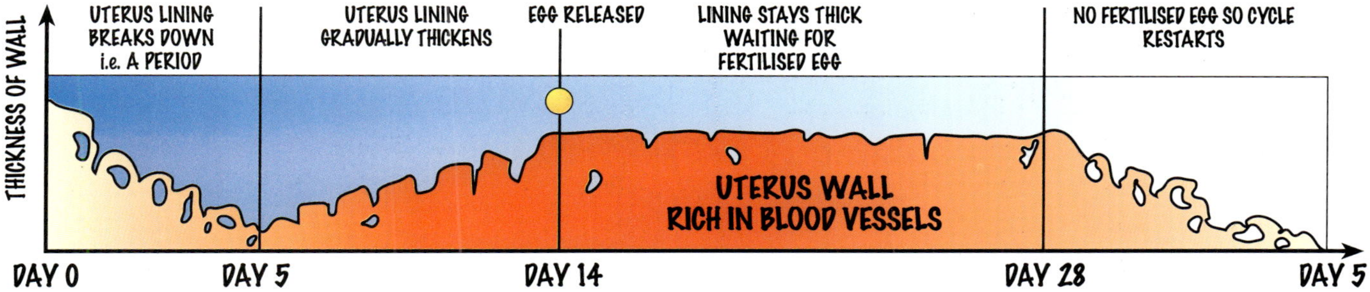

FERTILISATION

If fertilisation occurs the uterus wall remains intact and the fertilised egg implants (attaches to it). The sequence of events leading to this is ...

1. OVULATION (release of egg from ovary).
   (INTERCOURSE - sperm ejaculated into vagina).
2. FERTILISATION (fusion of sperm and egg).
3. CELL DIVISION (to form ball of cells, then embryo).
4. IMPLANTATION (into spongy lining of uterus).

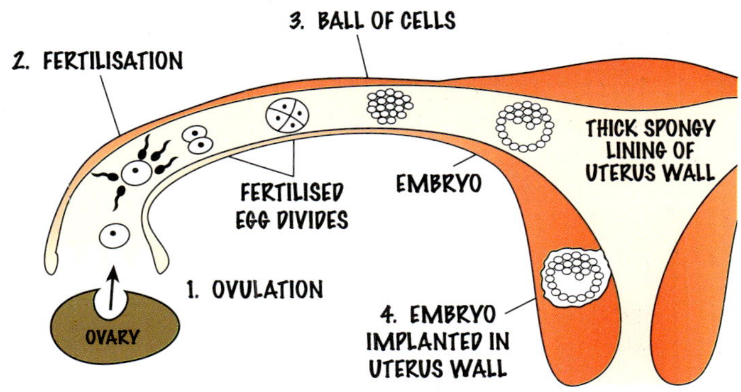

DEVELOPMENT OF THE FOETUS

After about 9 or 10 weeks the limbs are visible and the EMBRYO becomes a FOETUS.
The PLACENTA plays an important role during development ...

1. It brings the FOETAL blood into close contact with the mother's blood so that ...
   ... OXYGEN + FOOD pass into the foetal blood ...
   ... and CARBON DIOXIDE + WASTE pass into mum's blood.

NB. THE TWO BLOOD SUPPLIES DO NOT MIX.

2. It acts as a BARRIER to some harmful substances.

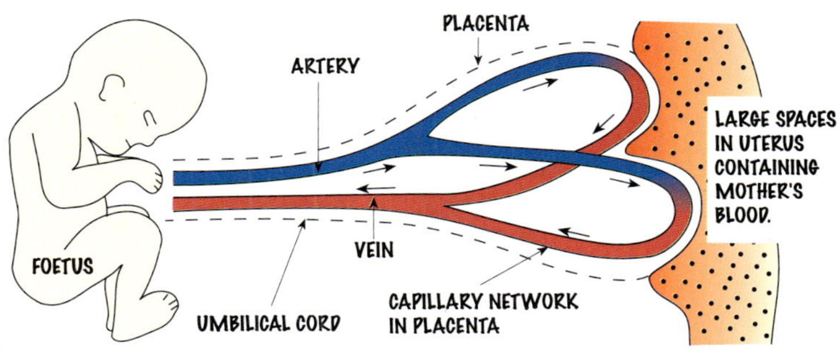

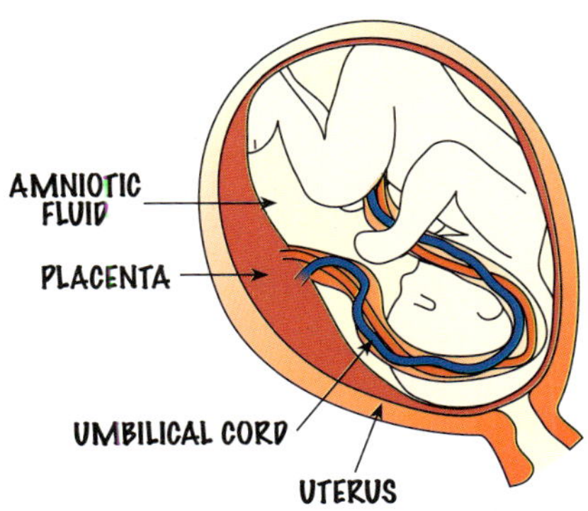

PROTECTION INSIDE THE UTERUS

- Inside the uterus the baby lives in a membranous sac ...
- ... filled with AMNIOTIC FLUID (the 'waters').
- This acts as a kind of 'shock absorber' ...
- ... to protect the baby from minor bumps.

1. Write a short essay to accompany the diagram showing the events leading to implantation of the embryo.
2. Think of a way of remembering the 4 stages, OVULATION, FERTILISATION, CELL DIVISION, and IMPLANTATION by using the first letters of their names.

TOBACCO

(See also page 9)

Tobacco is a legal substance which causes lots of health problems ...

- **LUNG CANCER** caused by substances in the tar of cigarette smoke.
- **LUNG INFECTIONS** due to cilia (see page 5) not working because of the tar.
- **EMPHYSEMA** air sacs damaged through coughing.
- **BRONCHITIS** irritation caused by smoke particles, and increased mucus ... ... allows infection to occur more easily.
- **ARTERIAL DISEASE** leading to heart attacks, strokes and even amputations.

ALCOHOL

In moderation this is relatively harmless. However alcohol abuse and dependency can cause serious problems ...

- **LIVER DAMAGE** Alcohol is a mild poison and causes parts of the liver ... ... to become fibrous and therefore useless.
- **BRAIN DAMAGE** Regular doses lead to increased brain cell death ... ... and a drop in mental performance e.g. memory.
- **IMPAIRED JUDGEMENT** This is while under the influence of alcohol. Acts of bravado or foolhardiness can have fatal effects.
- **ADDICTION** Extreme alcohol dependency can lead to regular days off, ... reduced performance at work, violence and money problems.

SOLVENTS

The vapour from various household substances is inhaled. Examples include glues and paints.
This practice can cause the following problems ...

- **HALLUCINATIONS** Users may lose their grip on reality.
- **PERSONALITY CHANGE** Users may start to display different personality traits.
- **DAMAGE TO ORGANS** Including Lungs, Brain, Liver and Kidneys. This is usually permanent.

OTHER DRUGS

- **HALLUCINOGENS** e.g. Ecstasy, L.S.D. These cause hallucinations, and in the case of Ecstasy the feeling of being full of energy which can lead to dehydration and collapse.
- **STIMULANTS** e.g. Amphetamine ('speed'), Methedrine. Users become psychologically dependent on the feelings of energy they can cause. Can cause change in personality.
- **DEPRESSANTS** e.g. Alcohol (see above), Barbiturates, depress the nervous system.
- **PAIN KILLERS** e.g. Heroin, Morphine. Addiction and complete collapse of personality and self-discipline.

1. Write a short essay on the "Evils of Tobacco".
2. Write a sensitive letter to a friend who is hooked on alcohol.
3. Design a poster on A4 paper to warn of the dangers of drugs. Aim it at 11 year olds.

BACTERIA AND VIRUSES

These are the two main types of microbe which may affect health.

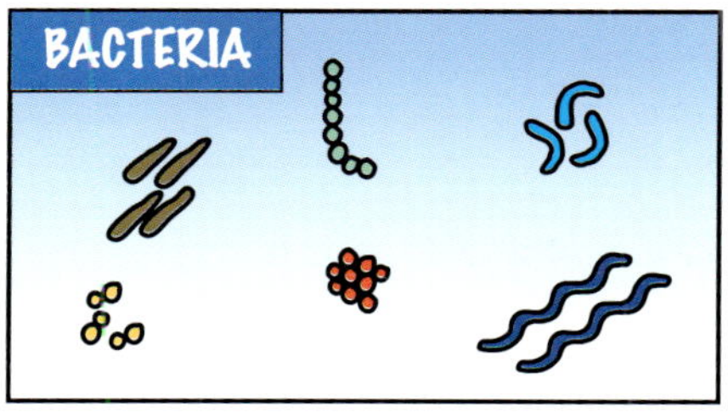

- VARY IN SHAPE
- ABOUT 1/1000TH mm
- NO DISTINCT NUCLEUS
- CELL WALL
- CAN REPRODUCE RAPIDLY
- CAN PRODUCE POISONS (TOXINS)
- KILLED BY ANTIBIOTICS.

A single bacterium

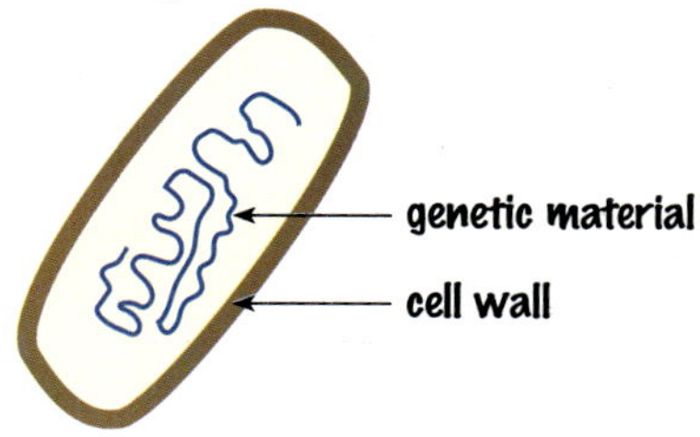

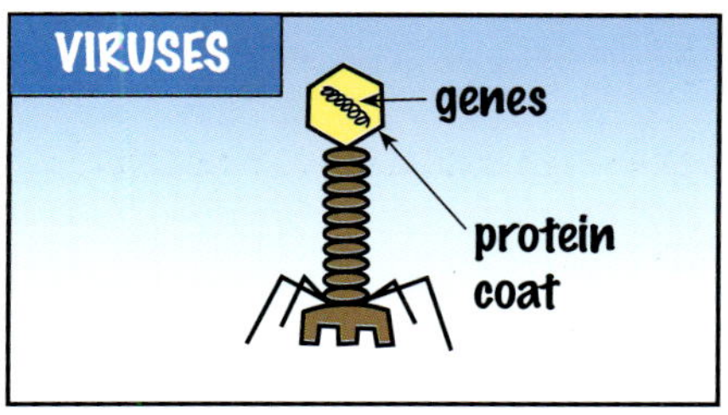

- VARY IN SHAPE
- ABOUT 1/10,000TH mm
- CONSISTS OF PROTEIN COAT SURROUNDING A FEW GENES
- ON BORDERLINE BETWEEN LIVING AND NON-LIVING
- CAN PRODUCE POISONS (TOXINS)
- CAN REPRODUCE RAPIDLY, BUT ONLY INSIDE LIVING CELLS CAUSING GREAT DAMAGE
- UNHARMED BY ANTIBIOTICS

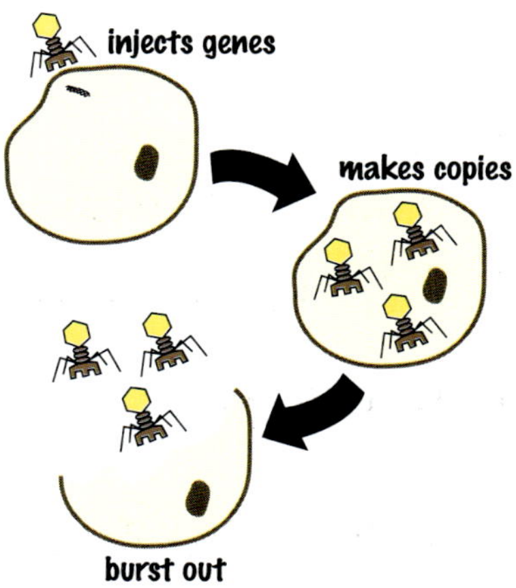

TYPICAL BACTERIAL DISEASES - Tetanus, cholera, tuberculosis.
TYPICAL VIRAL DISEASES - Colds, flu, measles, polio.

DEFENCE AGAINST INFECTION I - NATURAL IMMUNITY

- A microbe invades the body and starts to multiply ...
- ... causing the body's **WHITE CELLS** to multiply in response.
- Some white cells actually eat invading microbes ...
- ... but some produce **ANTIBODIES** and **ANTITOXINS** to attack the microbes.
- Once the white cells have been exposed to a particular microbe ...
- ... they can produce the relevant antibodies much quicker next time ...
- ... meaning that the individual now has **NATURAL IMMUNITY** to the disease.

DEFENCE AGAINST INFECTION II - IMMUNISATION

- Because it takes a while for white cells to produce the correct antibodies, ...
- ... a 'new' microbe can make a person very ill.
- However if the person is previously injected with some **DEAD MICROBES (IMMUNISED)** ...
- ... the white cells will make the appropriate antibodies even though there's no risk of illness.
- If subsequently this microbe invades the body, the white cells will already be "geared up".
- This means that antibodies will be produced more quickly, and the microbe destroyed.
- This type of immunity is called **ACTIVE ARTIFICIAL IMMUNITY**.

- Sometimes if a person hasn't been immunised he made need help against the microbe.
- This can be achieved by injecting antibodies directly into the bloodstream.
- These are made from horse blood serum, and confer **PASSIVE ARTIFICIAL IMMUNITY**.

1. Without looking at the page write down as many facts as you can about BACTERIA.
2. Without looking at the page write down as many facts as you can about VIRUSES.
3. Write a very short essay imagining that you are a virus which is just about to enter a human cell.

PHOTOSYNTHESIS

Photosynthesis means "making through light", and plants do make new BIOMASS as a result of light falling on them.

FOUR THINGS ARE NEEDED FOR PHOTOSYNTHESIS ...

1. LIGHT

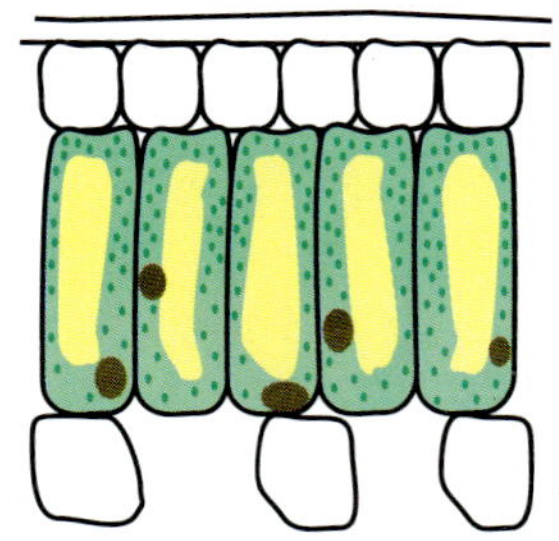

- Tall columnar PALISADE CELLS near the upper surface of the leaf are packed with chloroplasts to 'capture' light.

2. CARBON DIOXIDE

INCREASE IN BIOMASS

OXYGEN

Given off as a by product.

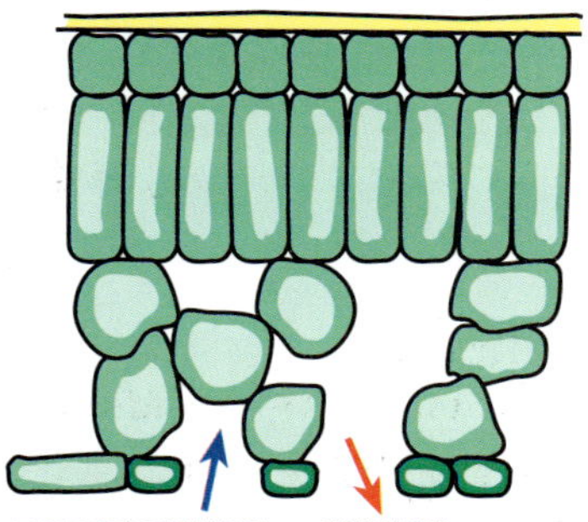

- These gases enter and leave via small holes on the under surface of the leaf called STOMATA.

3. WATER

- At the growing tips of the roots there are ROOT HAIR CELLS which ...

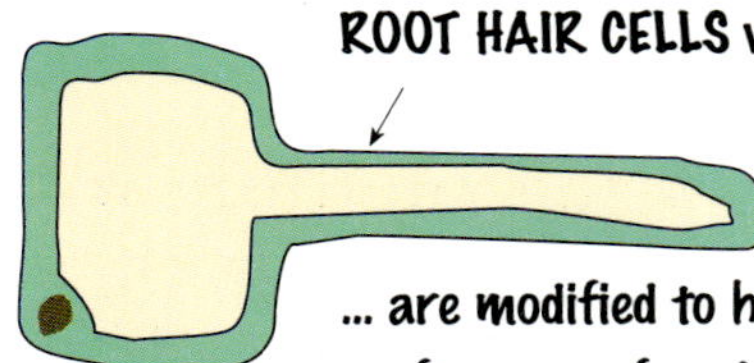

... are modified to have a large surface area for absorption of water and mineral salts.

4. CHLOROPHYLL, the green pigment in the chloroplasts is the special molecule which enables photosynthesis to occur.

THE WORD EQUATION

$$\text{CARBON DIOXIDE} + \text{WATER} \xrightarrow{\text{LIGHT ENERGY}} \text{GLUCOSE} + \text{OXYGEN}$$

- This GLUCOSE, is then all joined together to form long chains called STARCH.
- YOU MUST LEARN THIS EQUATION BY HEART! IT'S ABSOLUTELY VITAL.

THE NEED FOR MINERALS

Like water these are absorbed by the ROOT HAIR CELLS

NITROGEN	in the form of nitrates is needed to combine with carbohydrate produced in photosynthesis to form PROTEINS. These are used for growth (BIOMASS).
PHOSPHORUS	in the form of phosphates is needed in order that the plant can RESPIRE some of the glucose it makes, to meet its own energy needs.
POTASSIUM	is important in the chemical process of photosynthesis and also for the correct functioning of cell membranes.

1. Read this page very carefully and then close the book. Now try to design a poster on A4 paper which would explain what is needed for photosynthesis to occur. Remember, lots and lots of words are no good. It must be "snappy" and to the point.

PLANT REPRODUCTION 1

BASIC FLOWER STRUCTURE

- The MALE PARTS of the flower are ...
  ... the STAMENS.
- These consist of two parts ...
  The FILAMENT - which holds ...
  The ANTHER - which PRODUCES POLLEN.
- The FEMALE PART of the flower is ...
  ... the CARPEL.
- This is made up of three parts ...
  The STIGMA - which receives pollen grains.
  The STYLE - a tube of variable length.
  The OVARY - which contains the egg cell inside an OVULE.

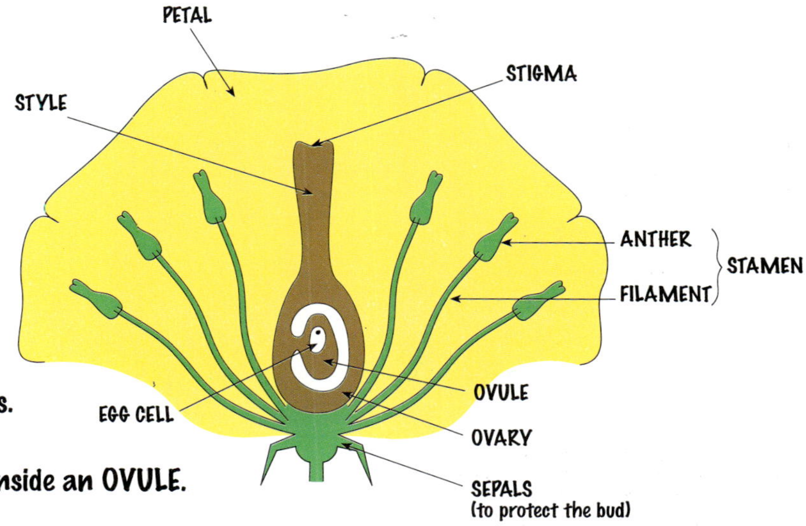

POLLINATION

Pollination is when pollen from the ANTHERS is deposited on a STIGMA. This is usually achieved by the WIND or by INSECTS and flowers are adapted accordingly.

WIND POLLINATED FLOWERS ...

- Dull green petals with no scent or nectaries.
- Anthers outside the flower on long dangly filaments.
- Feathery net-like stigma to catch pollen.
- Produce large amounts of light pollen.

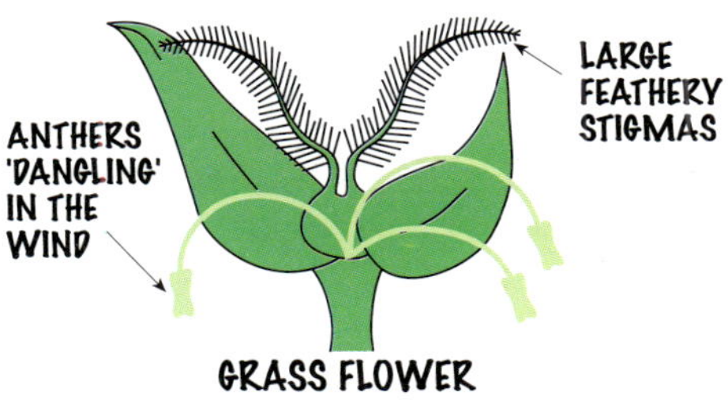

INSECT POLLINATED FLOWERS ...

- Brightly coloured, scented flowers with nectaries.
- Anthers inside the flower on the way to the nectaries.
- Sticky stigma inside the flower on the way to nectaries.
- Small amounts of large, sticky, pollen.

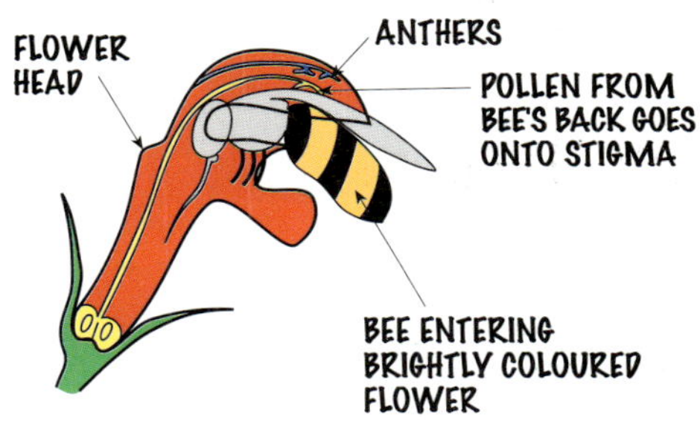

FERTILISATION

A CARPEL

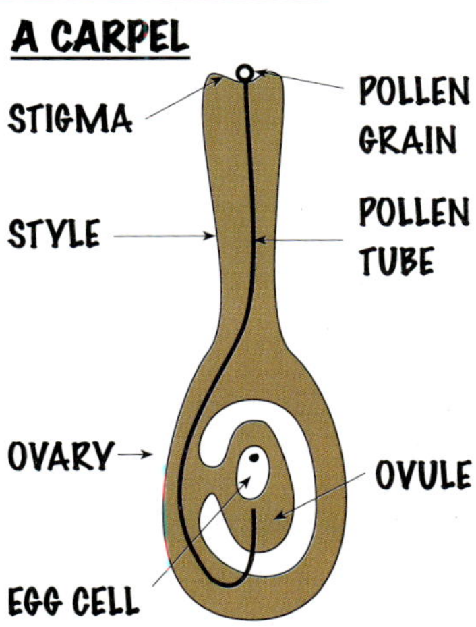

- Pollen first lands on the stigma. This is POLLINATION.
- A pollen tube then grows down the STYLE and into ...
- ... the OVARY and then OVULE until it reaches the egg cell.
- The male sex cell (gamete) then fuses with the female egg cell.
- This is FERTILISATION and results in the formation of a SEED ...
- ... from the OVULE. (See next page)

- A plant may CROSS-POLLINATE by transferring its pollen to the stigma ...
  ... of a FLOWER on a DIFFERENT PLANT.
- A plant may SELF-POLLINATE by transferring its pollen from the anthers to the stigma of the SAME FLOWER (or another flower on the SAME PLANT).

1. Without looking at the diagram above, try to sketch a flower showing the STIGMA, STYLE, OVARY, PETALS, SEPALS, ANTHERS and FILAMENTS.
2. Without looking at the diagram above, sketch a cross-section through a CARPEL showing a POLLEN TUBE entering the OVULE.

SEED FORMATION

After fertilisation, the **OVULE** becomes a **SEED** i.e. a miniature life support system to protect the embryo plant and sustain it in the early days after **GERMINATION**.

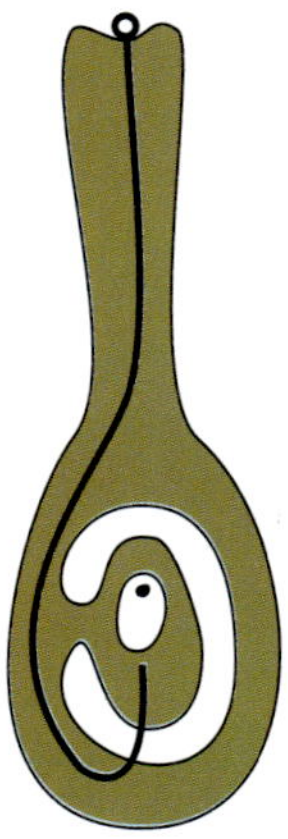

A carpel showing a pollen tube which has reached the ovule.

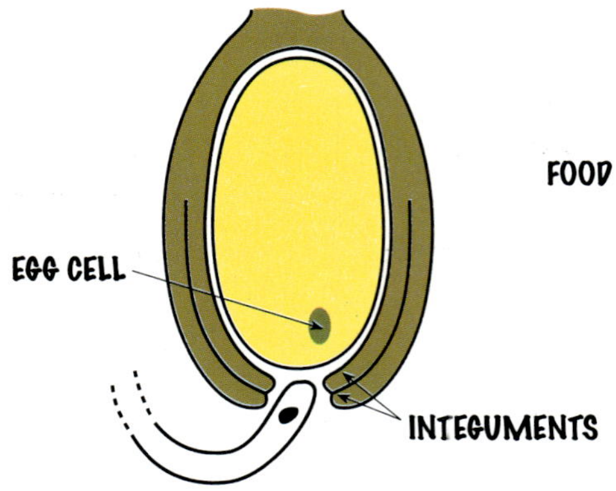

A close-up of the ovule showing the pollen tube entering it.

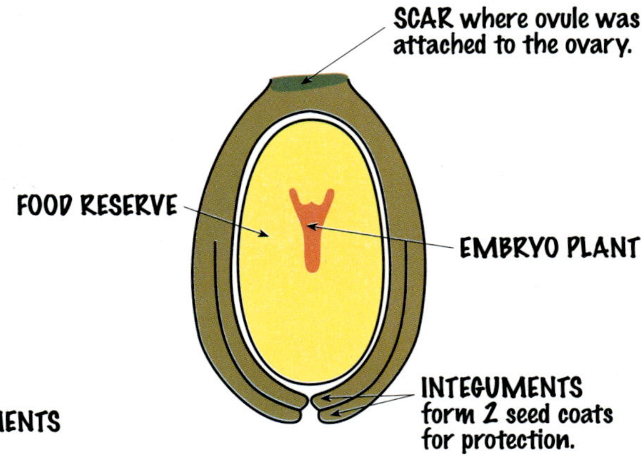

After fertilisation the ovule becomes a seed.

SEED DISPERSAL

- After **SEED FORMATION** the seeds are then **DISPERSED** (spread out) ...
- ... so that they can grow without **COMPETITION** from each other or the parent plant.
- Seeds can be dispersed by ... • **WIND** or • **ANIMALS** • Here are some examples.

Sycamore

Dandelion

Cleavers (goosegrass)

Hazelnut

GERMINATION

This is when a seed starts to grow into a new plant.

The full sequence of events in the reproduction of plants is ...

• 1. POLLINATION • 2. FERTILISATION • 3. SEED FORMATION • 4. SEED DISPERSAL • 5. GERMINATION

For **GERMINATION** to occur, the seed must have:-

- **ENOUGH WATER** ... to rehydrate the seed.
- **OXYGEN** ... for respiration to occur.
- the correct **TEMPERATURE** ... for enzymes to work properly.

1. Draw diagrams to illustrate any TWO methods of seed dispersal in addition to those shown above.
2. Draw brief sketches to illustrate the 5 stages leading to the development of a new plant.

WHAT VARIATION IS

Animals of different SPECIES have obvious differences, but ...

- ... even animals of the SAME SPECIES have (less obvious) differences. This is VARIATION.
- Look at the people in your class. You are all members of the same species but are all different.

THE CAUSES OF VARIATION

1. **GENETIC CAUSES** ... due purely to the GENES inherited from our parents.
   - Unless you have an IDENTICAL TWIN, your genes are UNIQUE to you.
   - Eye colour, hair colour, blood group etc. are all decided by the genes you inherit.
2. **ENVIRONMENTAL CAUSES** ... due to the circumstances and conditions of our UPBRINGING.
   - Your weight is an obvious example, as is the size of your muscles.
   - However, INTELLIGENCE, ATHLETICISM, and PERSONALITY are combinations of ...
     ... BOTH GENETIC AND ENVIRONMENTAL CAUSES ... as in fact are most things.
   - In PLANTS, environmental conditions have a huge effect on how the plant turns out ...
     ... more sunlight, more soil nutrients, and more water can make one plant twice as big as another.

SHOWING VARIATION ON BAR CHARTS

DISCONTINUOUS VARIATION

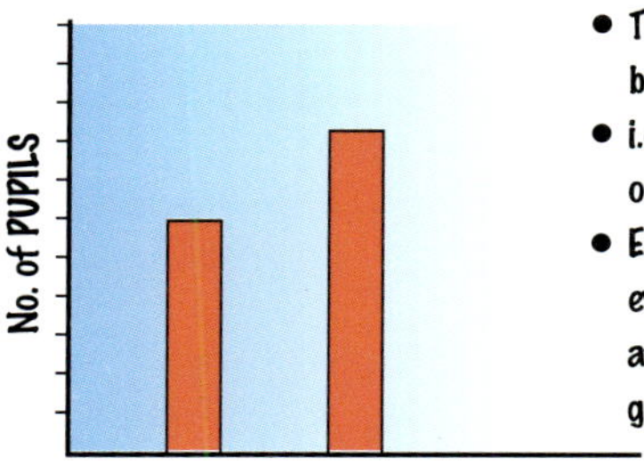

- This distribution is controlled by particular genes ...
- i.e. you've either got them or you haven't.
- Examples include ... eye colour, tongue rolling, attached ear lobes, blood groups, sex etc.

CONTINUOUS VARIATION

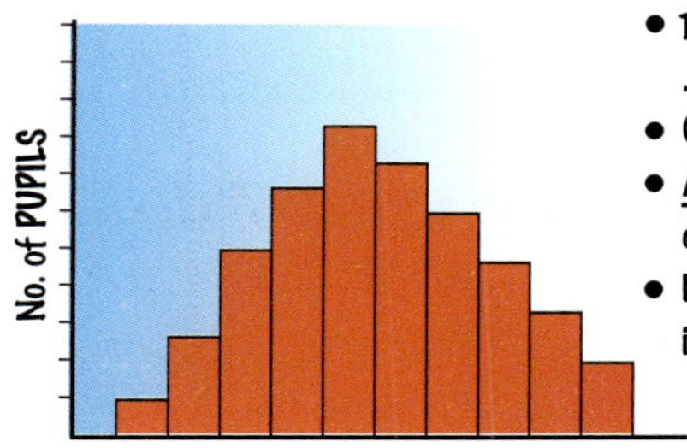

- This distribution is either ENVIRONMENTAL ... or controlled by lots of different genes.
- Or, it maybe a combination of both.
- A full range is always a characteristic of this type of variation.
- Examples include ... height, weight, intelligence, strength, speed, skin colour.

SELECTIVE BREEDING

NEW VARIETIES of organisms can be bred by taking advantage of VARIATION.

- Organisms with a desired characteristic, are bred with similar organisms ...
- ... resulting in offspring, some of which will have an EXAGGERATED VERSION OF THIS CHARACTERISTIC.
- These are then bred again, and so on, until the desired result is achieved.
- Many of our domestic livestock, fruit and vegetables would be unrecognisable to someone who lived three hundred years ago.

EXAMPLE OF GREEN VEGETABLES BRED FROM A COMMON ANCESTOR

It can take MANY, MANY GENERATIONS TO GET THE DESIRED RESULT!!

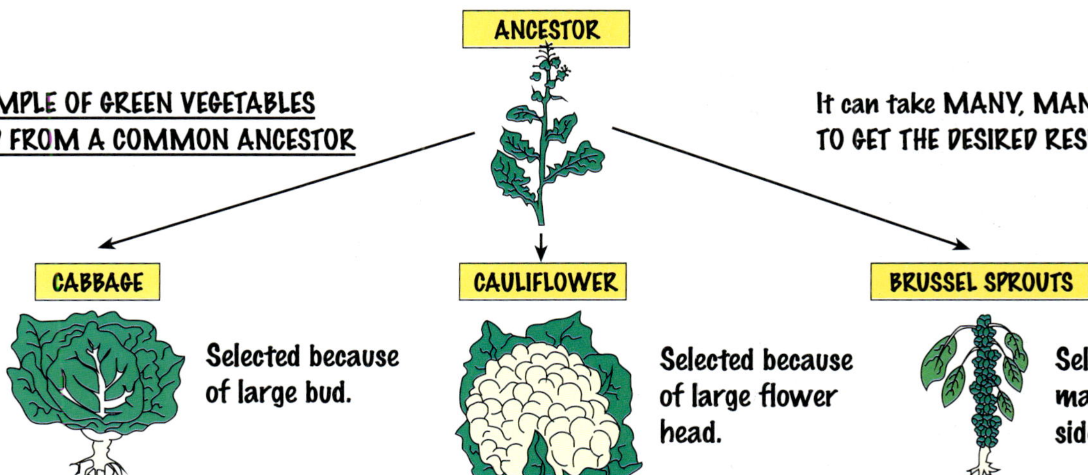

A selection of pea plants grew to the following heights in (cms): 57, 61, 63, 72, 58, 64, 90, 81, 87, 73, 76, 77, 71, 69, 81, 82, 78, 77, 76, 70, 68, 58, 76, 74, 74, 72, 74, 76, 87. Draw a BAR CHART to illustrate the distribution of heights.

Animals are divided into TWO main groups, the INVERTEBRATES and the VERTEBRATES.

THE INVERTEBRATES – Animals without backbones

These are the MAIN invertebrate groups ...

ANNELIDS – segmented worms
- Bodies divided into SEGMENTS.
- Each segment has BRISTLES.

MOLLUSCS
- Bodies UNSEGMENTED and ...
- ... very VARIABLE in shape!!

ARTHROPODS

CRUSTACEANS
- Body divided into 3 PARTS.
- Breathe through GILLS.
- External skeleton; jointed legs.

ARACHNIDS – Spiders and Scorpions
- Body divided into 2 PARTS.
- FOUR PAIRS OF LEGS: no wings.
- External skeleton; jointed legs.

INSECTS
- Body divided into 3 PARTS.
- THREE PAIRS OF LEGS: wings.
- External skeleton; jointed legs.

THE VERTEBRATES – animals with backbones

These are the FIVE vertebrate groups.

FISH
- Covered with SCALES.
- Have fins and GILLS.

AMPHIBIANS
- Breathe through MOIST SKIN and lungs.
- Need WATER TO BREED.

REPTILES
- Have DRY SCALY SKINS.
- Breathe only through LUNGS.

BIRDS
- Have FEATHERS and WINGS.
- Have BEAKS and no teeth.

MAMMALS
- Covered in HAIR (even us!)
- SUCKLE their young.

GREEN PLANTS

This doesn't include FUNGI because they haven't any chlorophyll.

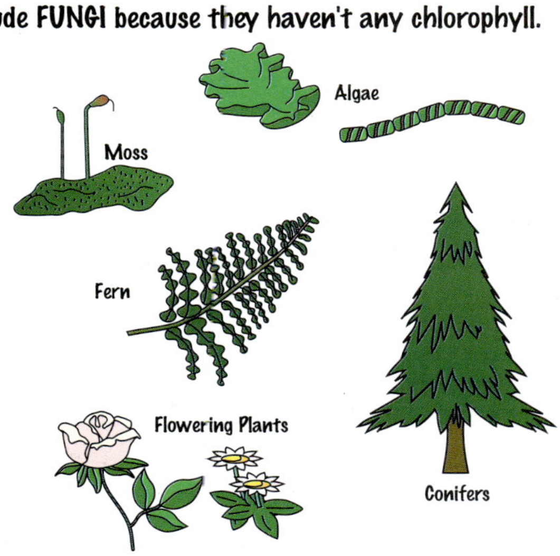

ALGAE
- NO roots, stems or leaves.
- Found in WATER.

MOSSES
- NO ROOTS; simple leaves and stem.
- Reproduce by SPORES.

FERNS
- HAS roots, stems and leaves.
- Reproduce by SPORES.

CONIFERS
- NEEDLE-LIKE leaves.
- Produce SEEDS ON CONES.

FLOWERING PLANTS
- Produce POLLEN and/or EGG CELLS.
- Seed develops from part of flower.

1. Try to find ONE other example of each of the INVERTEBRATE groups above. Explain the reasons of your choice.
2. Try to find ONE other example of each of the VERTEBRATE groups above. Explain the reasons of your choice.

Keys are quite a clever method of identifying organisms fairly quickly without having to check your specimen against pages and pages of organisms in a huge reference book. There are two methods ...

USING KEYS – Method One

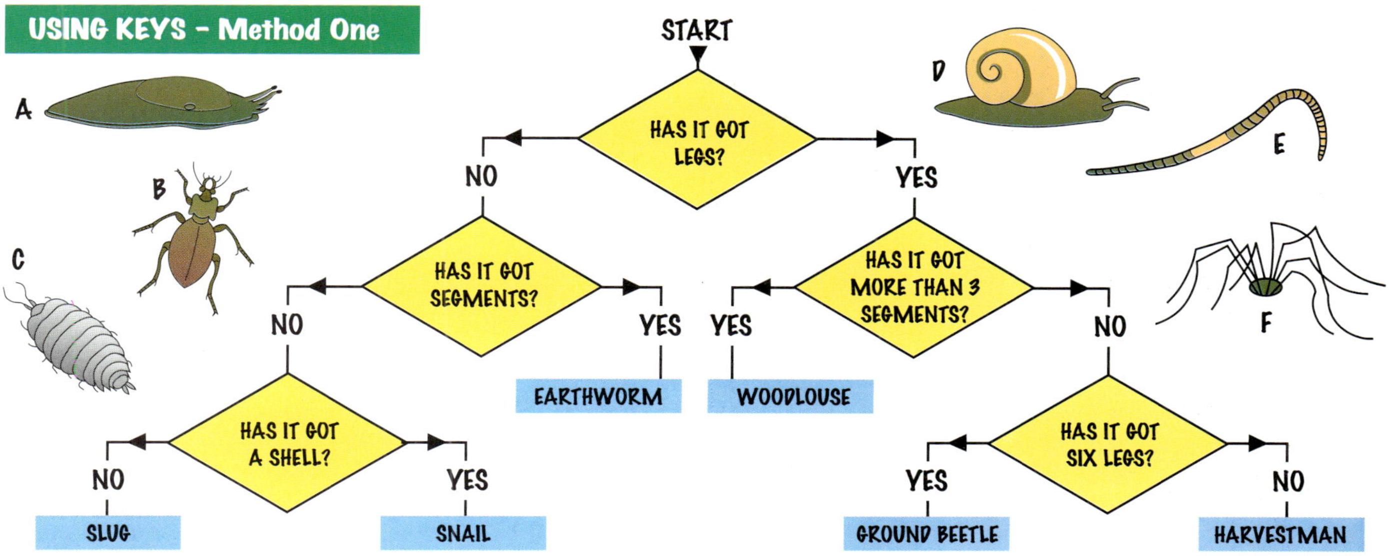

You would probably be asked to identify the garden organisms using this key ...

EXAMPLE:
- Take organism C, and go to the "START" ...
- Answer the question "Has it got legs?" – The answer is 'YES' so follow the "YES ARROW" ...
- Answer the next question "Has it got more than 3 segments?" – The answer is 'YES' ...
- ... so follow the "YES ARROW" and you can't go any further than **WOODLOUSE** i.e. the answer!!

So, now that you know C is a woodlouse, find out what the others are. (The answers are at the bottom of the page).

USING KEYS – Method Two

This one isn't often on exam papers but is the proper method!
Identify the invertebrates A – E using the key below ...

1	HAS LEGS	Go to 3
	HAS NO LEGS	Go to 2
2	HAS A SHELL	LYMNAEA
	HAS NO SHELL	TUBIFEX
3	HAS 3 PAIRS OF LEGS	Go to 4
	HAS MORE THAN 3 PAIRS OF LEGS	WATERLOUSE
4	HAS A TAIL	MAYFLY NYMPH
	HAS NO TAIL	WATER BEETLE

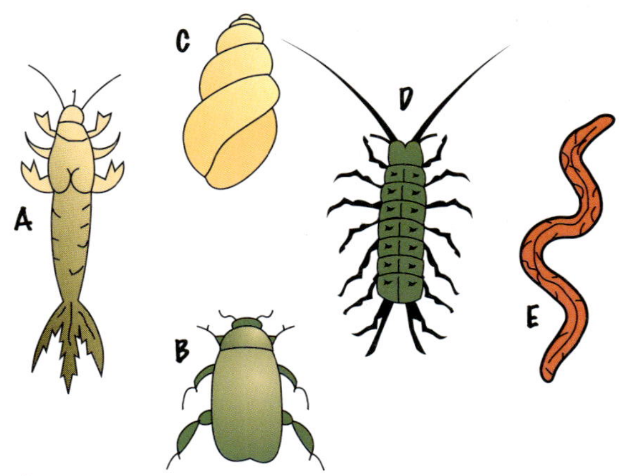

Just select an organism and answer the first question. Follow the instructions until you can't go any further. Also, remember that the same principle is used to identify plants using keys!

MAKING YOUR OWN KEY

Try this on your own class, using method 1 ...
- All you have to remember is that each question you design must split the group into TWO.
- So to begin with you could have "Is it a boy?" That should divide the class into two groups!
- Now you have to think of the next question to split the boys, and split them again and again ...
- ... until you identify each one individually .... then of course you have to do the same for the girls.

1. Design a key which would identify the VERTEBRATE animals on the page opposite.
2. Design a key using method 2 to identify the GREEN PLANTS on the page opposite.

A) SLUG B) GROUND BEETLE D) SNAIL E) EARTHWORM F) HARVESTMAN

ADAPTATION TO ENVIRONMENT

HABITATS

A habitat is the particular type of area in which an organism lives.
e.g. Woodlice live in dark damp areas beneath rotting organic material.
Sticklebacks live amongst weeds in ponds.
Mussels live around the low tide mark on exposed rocky beaches.

ADAPTATIONS

For an animal or plant to survive, it must be **WELL ADAPTED** to its **HABITAT**.
In other words, it has special features (**ADAPTATIONS**) which make it perfectly suited to where it lives ...

POLAR BEAR

- THICK LAYER OF FAT FOR INSULATION AND STORAGE.
- THICK WATERPROOF FUR FOR INSULATION.
- LARGE FEET TO DISTRIBUTE WEIGHT OVER SNOW AND ICE.
- ROUNDED SHAPE FOR RELATIVELY SMALL SURFACE AREA TO REDUCE HEAT LOSS.
- WHITE COLOUR TO BLEND IN WITH SURROUNDINGS.

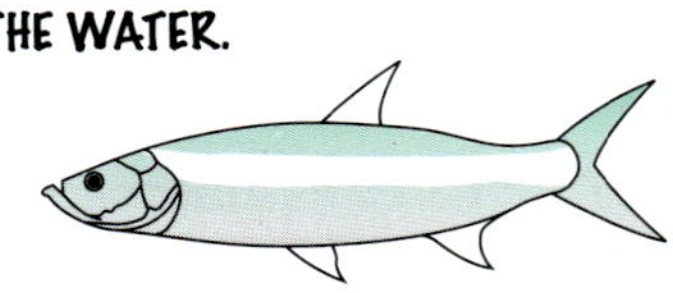

TROUT

- STREAMLINED SHAPE TO 'CUT THROUGH' THE WATER.
- MANY FINS TO CONTROL MOVEMENT IN THE WATER.

CACTUS

- LEAVES ARE REDUCED TO SPINES TO REDUCE WATER LOSS ...
- ... AND TO KEEP GRAZING ANIMALS AWAY.
- SWOLLEN STEM STORES WATER.
- STOMATA ARE IN DEPRESSIONS or PITS TO REDUCE WATER LOSS IN WINDY CONDITIONS.
- WIDESPREADING ROOTS TO INCREASE ABSORPTION AREA.

SPARROW HAWK

- STREAMLINED SHAPE AND POWERFUL WING MUSCLES ENABLE IT TO REACH HIGH SPEEDS TO CATCH PREY.
- EXCELLENT EYESIGHT FOR HUNTING.
- POWERFUL BEAK AND TALONS ('CLAWS') FOR SEIZING PREY.

Even though an organism's adaptations may not be obvious, believe me ...

ALL LIVING ORGANISMS ARE ADAPTED TO THE HABITAT IN WHICH THEY LIVE.

DAILY AND SEASONAL ADAPTATIONS

Some organisms respond to **PERIODIC CHANGES IN THEIR ENVIRONMENT.**

EXAMPLES OF ADAPTATION TO DAILY CHANGE

1. Stomata on leaves close at night to prevent water loss.
2. Some flowers close at night to prevent damage due to fall in temperature.
3. Many animals sleep during the day to avoid being easily seen by predators.

EXAMPLES OF ADAPTATION TO SEASONAL CHANGE

1. Many trees shed leaves in winter to reduce the amount of water they lose when the ground is frozen.
2. Many mammals increase the thickness of their coat as winter approaches.
3. The skin of humans darkens on exposure to sunlight to protect them from ultra-violet radiation.

1. Write down THREE more habitats and suggest organisms which may live there.
2. Select FOUR more organisms which show particularly good adaptations to their environment. Explain how these adaptations help them.

FOOD WEBS

Food webs show the FEEDING RELATIONSHIPS in a particular environment.
Arrows show who is eating whom and the direction of energy flow in the web.

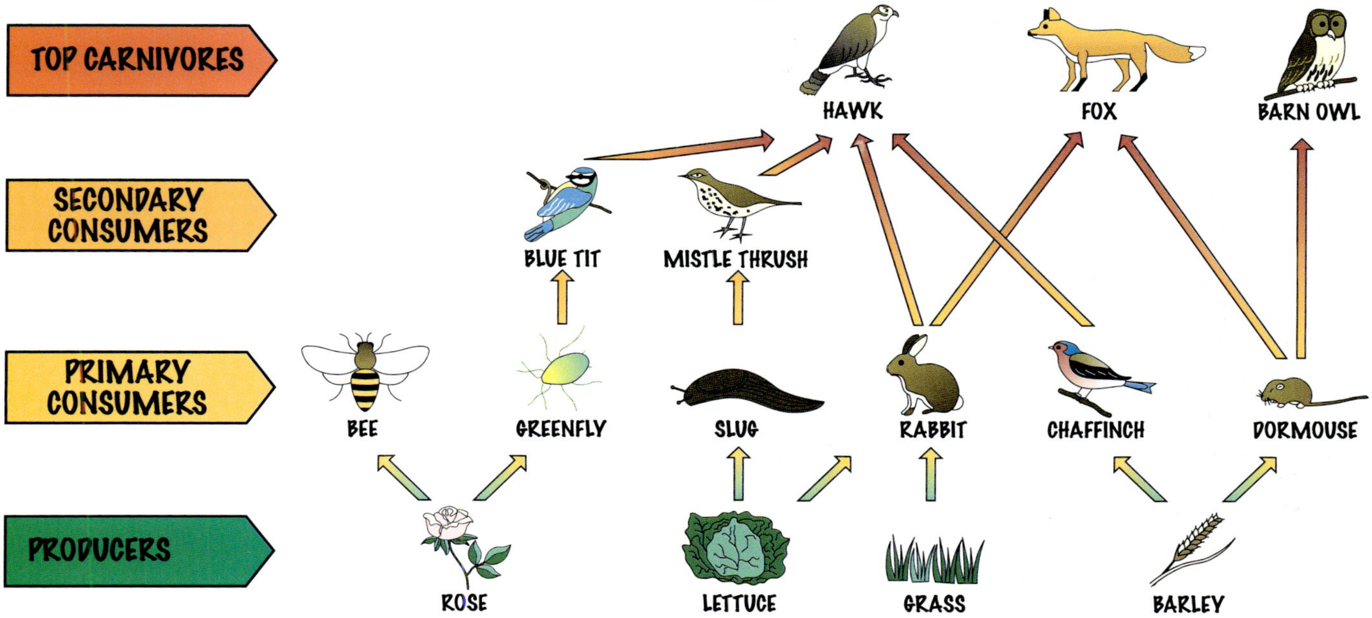

- All the **PRIMARY CONSUMERS** are **HERBIVORES** i.e. they only eat plants.
- All the **SECONDARY CONSUMERS** are **CARNIVORES** i.e. they only eat animals, not plants.
- The BLUE TIT would also eat SEEDS as well as GREENFLY and so is called an **OMNIVORE** (meat and plants).
- Missing from this diagram are the **DECOMPOSERS** which release the nutrients from dead material by breaking it down.

BREAKING THE LINKS

Because everything in the food web is so independent, ...
... IF ONE ORGANISM DIES MANY OTHERS CAN BE AFFECTED!!
In the food web above, consider what happen if all the rabbits died!? ...

- ... Well, ... the LETTUCE and the GRASS could well start to INCREASE ...
- ... but the HAWKS and FOXES may reduce in number due to lack of food, UNLESS ...
- ... they started eating more BLUE TITS, THRUSHES and CHAFFINCHES in the case of the HAWK, or ...
- ... more DORMICE in the case of FOXES.
- Also, the increase in LETTUCE may cause a big increase in SLUGS and therefore THRUSHES!
  AS YOU CAN SEE, THE MORE COMPLEX THE FOOD WEB, THE GREATER THE NUMBER OF PERMUTATIONS.

FOOD CHAINS

Besides energy and biomass, other substances can pass along food chains.

e.g. LETTUCE SLUGS MISTLE THRUSHES HAWKS

- If a TOXIN (Poison) gets into the food chain it can be passed along from organism to organism.
- However, as it passes along the chain it becomes more concntrated and may kill the TOP CARNIVORE.

1. List as many PRODUCERS as you can think of in 30 seconds.
2. List as many PRIMARY CONSUMERS as you can think of in 30 seconds.
3. List as many SECONDARY CONSUMERS as you can think of in 30 seconds.
4. Pick at least FOUR of each of the above and make your own FOOD WEB.

PYRAMIDS OF NUMBERS

QUANTIFYING FOOD CHAINS

Energy from the Sun gets passed along food chains, ...
... but some energy is 'used' (or transferred) at each stage of the chain.
i.e. in a food chain of **GRASS** ⟶ **RABBITS** ⟶ **FOX**, all the energy which the rabbits get from the grass is NOT PASSED ON TO THE FOX, since the rabbit transfers some of this energy into movement and heat energy etc. This usually means that as we move up from one level to the next level in a food chain, the number of organisms <u>decreases</u> quite dramatically.

PYRAMIDS OF NUMBERS

This decrease in numbers can be shown using PYRAMIDS OF NUMBERS to represent the organisms in the food chain.

e.g. 1. from the food web overleaf ...

GRASS ⇨ RABBITS ⇨ FOX

e.g. 2. Also from the food web overleaf ...

BARLEY ⇨ DORMOUSE ⇨ BARN OWL

These PYRAMIDS OF NUMBERS can be drawn to SCALE, but in practice they're usually not.
However they still give a good idea of how much food is required from the level below by the level above (if you know what I mean!).

"ODD" PYRAMIDS OF NUMBERS

Lets have a look at two more food chains from the food web overleaf.

e.g. 3.

LETTUCE ⇨ SLUG ⇨ MISTLE THRUSH ⇨ HAWK

This happens because the lettuces are large organisms compared to the slugs.

e.g. 4.

ROSE ⇨ GREENFLY ⇨ BLUE TIT ⇨ HAWK

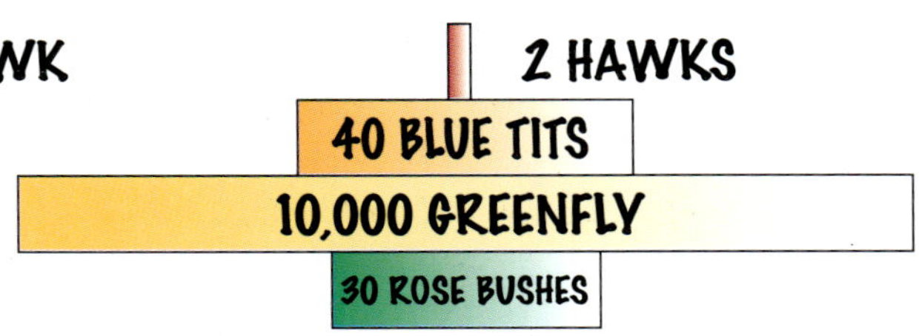

This happens because the Rose bushes are very large organisms compared to the Greenfly.

1. Draw a pyramid of numbers for BARLEY ⟶ CHAFFINCH ⟶ HAWK.
2. Draw a pyramid of numbers for GRASS ⟶ RABBIT ⟶ HAWK.
3. Draw a pyramid of numbers for ROSE ⟶ BEE.
4. Draw a pyramid of numbers for OAK TREE ⟶ CATERPILLAR ⟶ BLUE TIT.

COMPETITION AND SURVIVAL

THE SIZE OF POPULATIONS

Living organisms generally produce lots of offspring, which then also reproduce. However the population of a particular **SPECIES** doesn't just keep on rising!! The size of a population is controlled by three major factors.

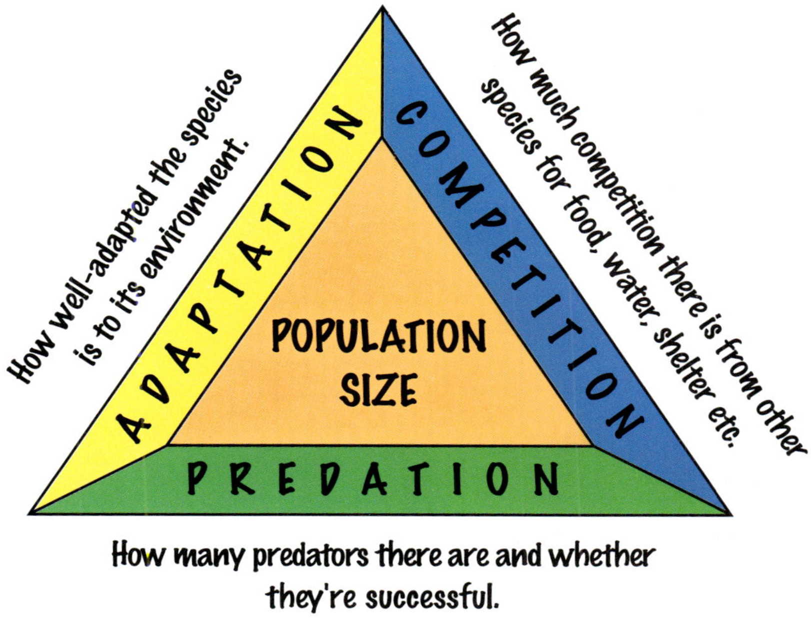

PREDATOR/PREY CYCLES

The numbers of **PREDATOR** species (the hunters) is closely linked to the numbers of their **PREY** (the hunted) and vice versa. Take a look at the diagram ...

- An increase in the food supply of the HARES, ...
- ... results in an INCREASE in the HARE POPULATION.
- This provides more food for the LYNX which ...
- ... results in an INCREASE in the LYNX POPULATION.
- However more LYNX results in LESS HARES ...
- ... which in time results in LESS LYNX again!!!
- These fluctuating population sizes are typical of a predator/prey relationship.

A classic example - LYNX AND HARES CYCLE

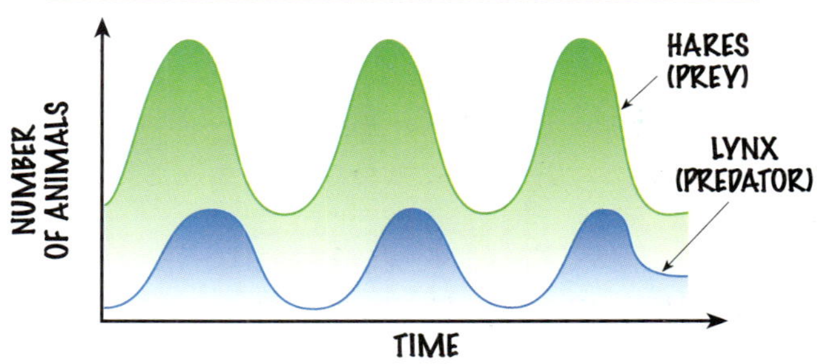

ADAPTATION AND COMPETITION

- Life is really quite a struggle for survival, ...
- ... and organisms which are well-adapted to their environment ...
- ... will compete successfully, and are more likely to survive ...
- ... and contribute relatively more offspring to the next generation.

The animals and plants in the world today are here because they are the descendants of successful ancestors. In other words, their ancestors were **WELL ADAPTED** to their environment and so survived and bred successfully for generation after generation.

Think of a species which is well adapted to its environment, then decide with which species it has to compete. Finally decide whether any predators are involved, or if the animal you have chosen is a predator, decide which prey it would depend on. Repeat this exercise for three more animals.

SUMMARY QUESTIONS

1 The rabbit in the diagram is alive. It MOVES, REPRODUCES, GROWS, and EATS.
Which 3 other things does it do which all living things do?

2 Name two types of tissue which would be present in the heart.

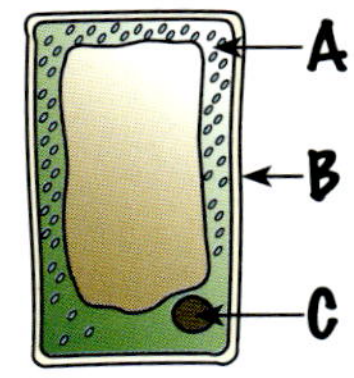

3 a) On the diagram of the plant cell shown alongside, what are the structures labelled A, B and C.

b) Name two structures which are found in plant cells but not animal cells.

c) How is the sperm cell shown in the diagram alongside, well adapted to its function?

d) Describe a cell which you think is specially designed to have a large surface area.

4 a) Draw lines to connect the three constituents of food to their uses and their sources. One has been done for you.

MEAT AND FISH	PROTEIN	STORED ENERGY
BUTTER AND LARD	CARBOHYDRATES	GROWTH AND REPAIR
BREAD AND POTATOES	FAT	IMMEDIATE ENERGY

b) Describe how the diets of an OFFICE WORKER and a HEAVY MANUAL WORKER <u>should</u> differ.

c) When would <u>extra</u> protein be required in the diet?

5 a) For what purpose is the canine tooth shown alongside adapted?

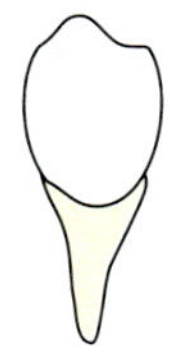

CANINE TOOTH

b) Why do we need to chew food?

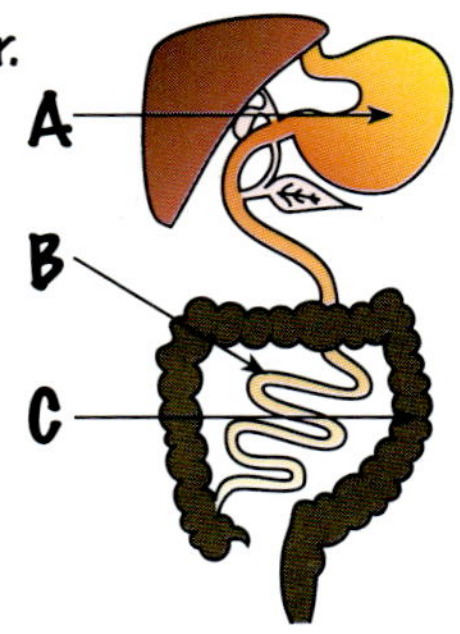

DIGESTIVE SYSTEM

6 a) Name the three parts labelled A, B and C on the diagram of the digestive system.

b) Explain what each of these parts does.

7 a) Why is the LEFT side of the heart more muscular than the right side?

b) In the diagram of the circulation, what is indicated by the two different colours?

c) Name two substances which pass <u>from</u> blood capillaries into the body cells.

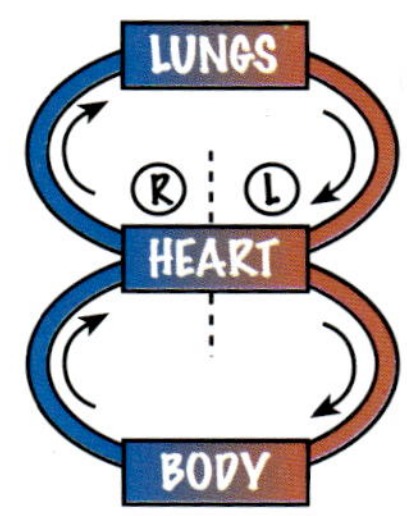

8 a) Describe two differences between 'AIR BREATHED IN' and 'AIR BREATHED OUT'.

b) Describe 4 ways in which the lungs are well adapted for gas exchange.

c) Explain why the air sac shown is now less efficient than it once was.

DAMAGED AIR SAC

9 a) Write down a WORD equation for respiration.

b) Which molecule in this equation contains the energy which the cell needs?

10 a) Name two functions of the skeleton?

b) What type of joint is indicated by the letter A on the diagram?

c) What type of joint is indicated by the letter B on the diagram?

d) Explain how the muscles of the arm work in order to a) bend the arm, and b) straighten the arm.

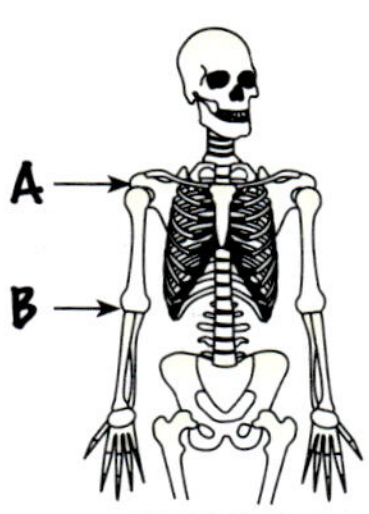

SKELETON

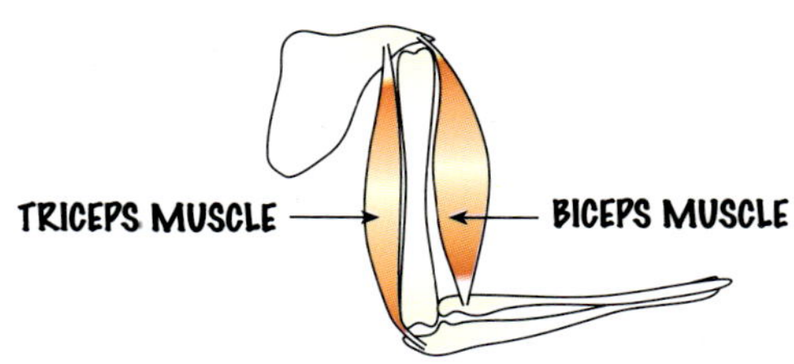

11 a) Arrange the following into the order in which they occur during human reproduction.

FERTILISATION | IMPLANTATION | CELL DIVISION | OVULATION

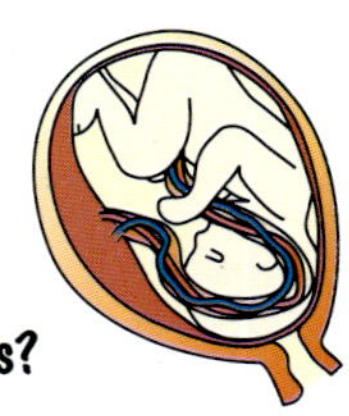

FOETUS IN UTERUS

b) Which two substances pass from the mother's blood across the placenta into the blood of the foetus?

c) The baby is enclosed inside a membrane filled with fluid. What is the purpose of this fluid?

12 a) Match the characteristics to Bacteria and Viruses. One has been done for you.

BACTERIA	ABOUT 1/1000th mm
VIRUSES	HAS A PROTEIN COAT
	KILLED BY ANTIBIOTICS
	ABOUT 1/10,000th mm

b) What is NATURAL IMMUNITY? How does the body acquire it?

13 a) Which TWO gases are exchanged during photosynthesis?

b) How is the leaf well adapted to enable this gas exchange?

c) Write a WORD equation for the process of photosynthesis.

14 a) Match the letters A, B and C opposite to the following descriptions.

Structures where pollen is produced	
Structures where seeds are produced	
Where pollination occurs	

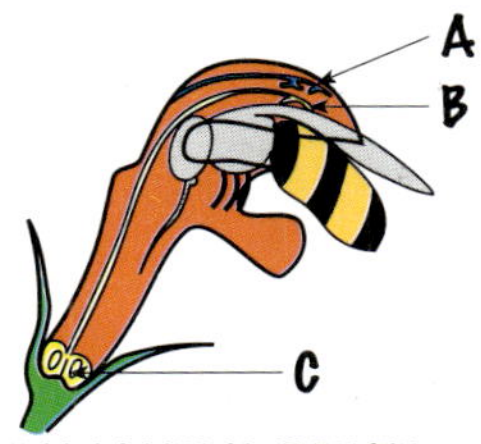

BEE ENTERING FLOWER

b) Explain the difference between CROSS-POLLINATION and SELF-POLLINATION.

c) Describe TWO characteristics of wind pollinated plants.

d) Explain how the seeds below are DISPERSED in different ways.

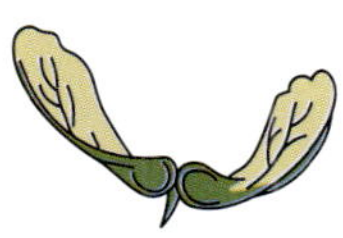
SYCAMORE

GOOSEGRASS

e) Arrange the following into the order in which they occur during plant reproduction.

SEED DISPERSAL	GERMINATION	SEED FORMATION	POLLINATION	FERTILSATION

15 The bar chart shows a certain type of distribution.

Which TWO of the following characteristics would produce this type of distribution?

EYE COLOUR, HEIGHT, BLOOD GROUPS, SEX, INTELLIGENCE

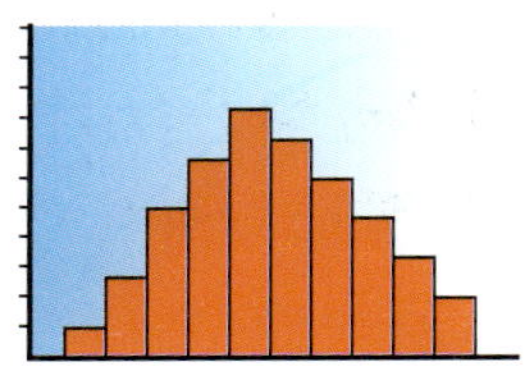

16 a) Draw lines to indicate whether the following animal groups are VERTEBRATES or INVERTEBRATES. One has been done for you.

BIRDS	VERTEBRATES	MOLLUSCS
INSECTS	INVERTEBRATES	MAMMALS
REPTILES		ARACHNIDS

b) Devise a 'branching' key to identify the organisms opposite.

c) Now use the 'proper' method of paired questions to identify the animals.

d) Describe 3 ways in which <u>each</u> organism is adapted to its environment.

e) Give <u>one</u> example of how an organism can adapt to seasonal change.

17 a) Create a food chain consisting of four organisms, and label the herbivore.

b) Create a food web consisting of 2 producers, 3 primary consumers, and 2 secondary consumers.

c) Construct a pyramid of numbers for the food chain you have produced in part (a).

d) Why do some pyramids of numbers turn out to be very unpyramid-like?

18 a) What is a predator?

b) Describe what is happening in this graph opposite.

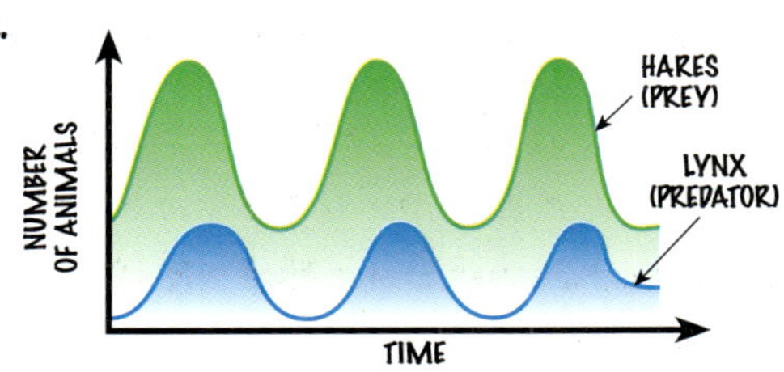

MATERIALS AND THEIR PROPERTIES I

It is very important that if a MATERIAL is used for a PARTICULAR JOB, it has PROPERTIES WHICH MAKE IT SUITABLE for that job. Here are some common properties.

HARDNESS

- A HARD MATERIAL CANNOT have it's SHAPE CHANGED VERY EASILY and will DENT or SCRATCH a SOFTER MATERIAL.
- Examples include DIAMOND and STEEL.

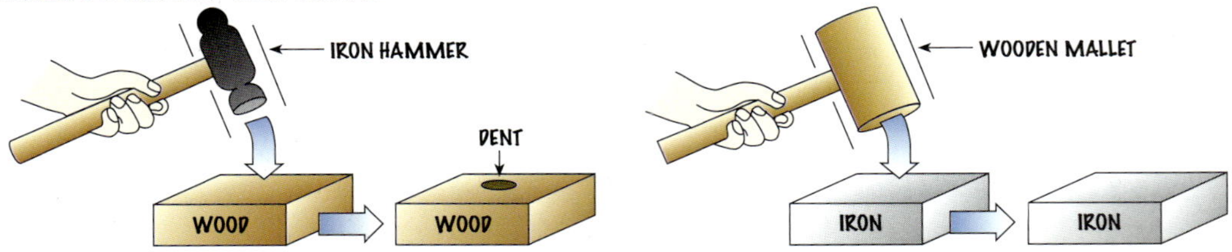

IRON MAKES A DENT IN WOOD ... while ... WOOD MAKES NO DENT IN IRON

STRENGTH

- A STRONG MATERIAL is VERY DIFFICULT to BREAK when it is STRETCHED OR SQUEEZED.
- Examples include REINFORCED CONCRETE and STEEL.

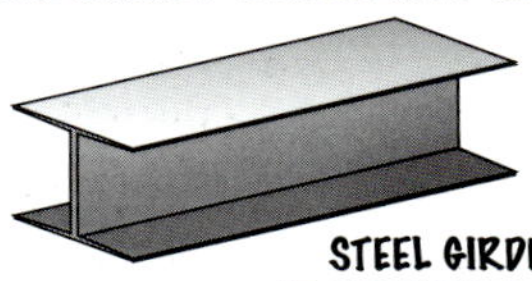

STEEL GIRDER TO SUPPORT A ROOF

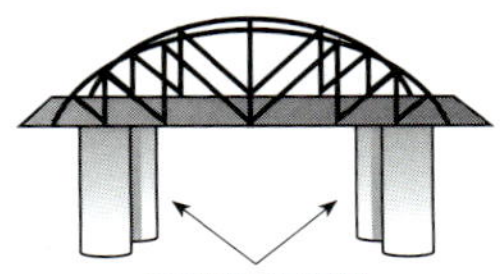

REINFORCED CONCRETE PILLARS

FLEXIBILITY

- A FLEXIBLE MATERIAL can be BENT EASILY without BREAKING.
- Examples include RUBBER and most PLASTICS.

CREDIT CARD

ELASTICITY

- An ELASTIC MATERIAL can be STRETCHED but will GO BACK TO ITS ORIGINAL SHAPE when it is released.
- Examples include ELASTIC BANDS and SPRINGS.

ATTRACTION TO A MAGNET

- A FEW MATERIALS (IRON and STEEL) are attracted to a magnet while ...
- ... ALL OTHER MATERIALS ARE NOT ATTRACTED.

IRON IS ATTRACTED TO THE MAGNET ... while ... PLASTIC AND ALL OTHER MATERIALS ARE NOT

TOUGHNESS AND BRITTLENESS

- A TOUGH MATERIAL is DIFFICULT to BREAK by HITTING IT with another object while ...
- ... a BRITTLE MATERIAL BREAKS EASILY if it is HIT.

Examples of tough materials:-	Examples of brittle materials:-
WOOD, MOST METALS AND SOME PLASTICS	CERAMICS, GLASS AND SOME PLASTICS

For each of the characteristics above make a list of as many household objects as you can which have that particular characteristic. List separately those objects which show three or more of these characteristics.

THERMAL CONDUCTORS AND INSULATORS

A MATERIAL which allows HEAT to pass through it easily is a THERMAL CONDUCTOR while ...
... a MATERIAL which DOESN'T is called a non-conductor or THERMAL INSULATOR.

Here's a simple experiment to show whether a material is a conductor or an insulator ...

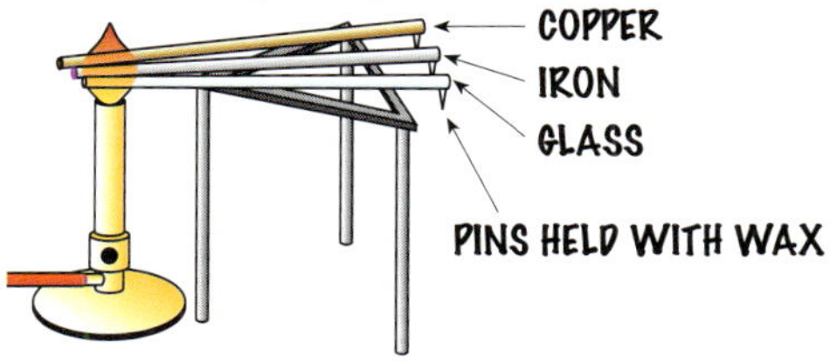

- The PIN FALLS off the COPPER ROD FIRST ...
- ... showing that it's the BEST CONDUCTOR.
- The pin on the IRON ROD falls next.

- The PIN STAYS ON THE GLASS ROD ...
- ... showing that it is an INSULATOR.

GOOD CONDUCTORS
- ALL METALS especially COPPER and ALUMINIUM

GOOD INSULATORS
- GLASS
- WOOD
- PLASTIC
- AIR

ALL THREE RODS ARE HEATED EQUALLY BY A BUNSEN BURNER.

An example of an everyday object which makes use of TWO materials, one a CONDUCTOR and the other an INSULATOR is the SAUCEPAN.

- The PAN is made from a CONDUCTOR ...
- ... COPPER or ALUMINIUM ...
- ... which TRANSFERS HEAT ...
- ... to the INSIDE of the PAN.

- The HANDLE is made from an INSULATOR ...
- ... PLASTIC or WOOD ...
- ... which doesn't TRANSFER HEAT UP THE HANDLE ...
- ... so it is safe to touch and hold.

ELECTRICAL CONDUCTORS AND INSULATORS

A MATERIAL that allows ELECTRICITY to flow through it is an ELECTRICAL CONDUCTOR while ...
... a MATERIAL THAT DOESN'T is called an ELECTRICAL INSULATOR.

Here's a simple experiment to show whether a material is a conductor or an insulator ...

GOOD CONDUCTORS
- ALL METALS especially COPPER.
- CARBON (graphite).

GOOD INSULATORS
- GLASS
- WOOD
- PLASTIC
- AIR
- RUSTY METALS

THE MATERIAL IS PLACED TOUCHING BOTH BARE WIRES, TO TRY TO COMPLETE THE CIRCUIT.

Nearly all ELECTRICAL APPLIANCES are supplied with electricity by a CABLE connected to a THREE-PIN PLUG, both of which make use of materials that are CONDUCTORS and INSULATORS.

- The CABLE is made from an INSULATOR ...
- ... PLASTIC or RUBBER.

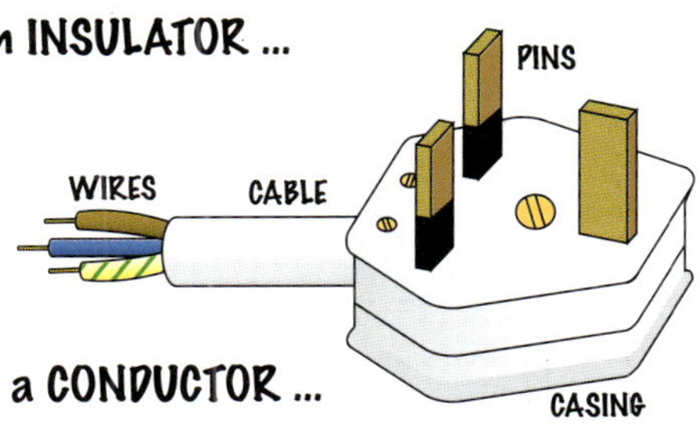

- The PINS are made from a CONDUCTOR ...
- ... BRASS.

- The WIRES are made from a CONDUCTOR ...
- ... COPPER.

- The CASING is made from an INSULATOR ...
- ... PLASTIC.

1. What is a thermal conductor?
2. Draw a simple diagram to show that some materials conduct heat while others don't.
3. Name TWO thermal conductors and TWO thermal insulators.
4. What is an electrical conductor?
5. Draw a simple diagram to show that some materials conduct electricity while others don't.
6. Name TWO electrical conductors and TWO electrical insulators.

• EVERYTHING is made up of MATTER which exists as either SOLID, LIQUID or GAS. (The 3 states of matter).

Let's consider some of the PROPERTIES of SOLIDS, LIQUIDS and GASES.

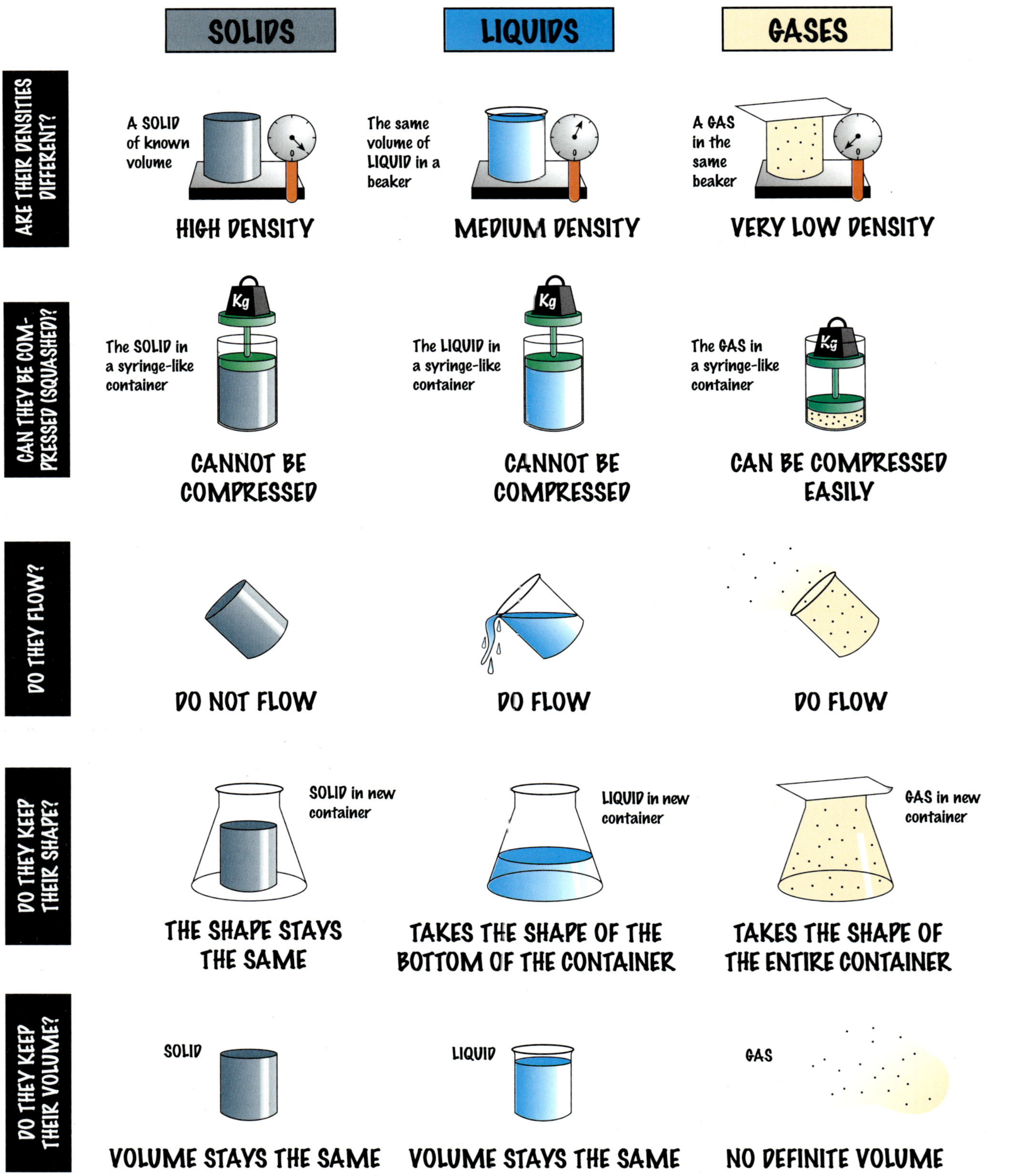

1. What are the three states of matter?

2. Explain using diagrams how the following properties are different for each state: a) their density, b) their ability to be compressed, c) their ability to flow, d) their ability to keep their shape and e) their ability to keep their volume.

- ALL SOLIDS, LIQUIDS and GASES are made up of VERY SMALL PARTICLES, ...
- ... far too small for the eye to see ...
- ... which are ALWAYS MOVING.

SOLIDS

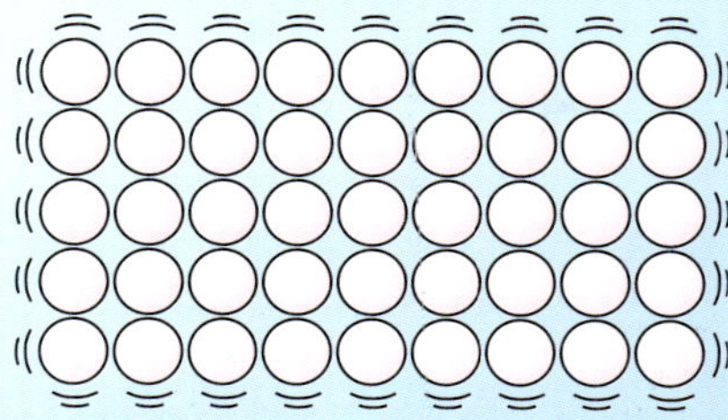

Particles are ...
- VERY CLOSE TOGETHER and ...
- ... EACH PARTICLE exerts a LARGE FORCE OF ATTRACTION ...
- ... on every OTHER PARTICLE.

Particles can ...
- ONLY VIBRATE (move to and fro) ...
- ... about their NORMAL POSITION which doesn't change.

LIQUIDS

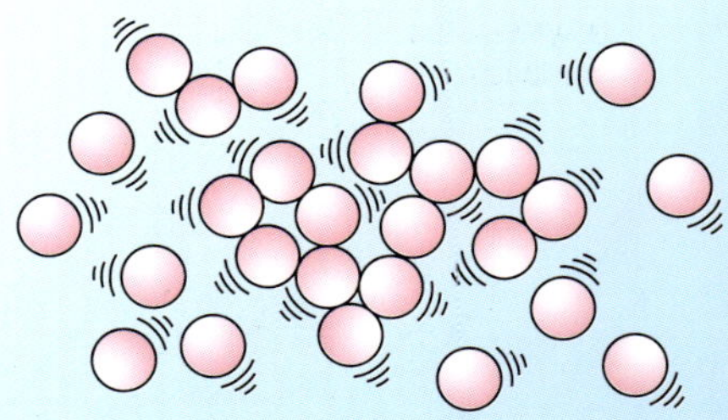

Particles are ...
- CLOSE TOGETHER and ...
- ... EACH PARTICLE exerts a SMALLER FORCE OF ATTRACTION ...
- ... on every OTHER PARTICLE.

Particles can ...
- MOVE AROUND ...
- ... in ANY DIRECTION within the liquid.

GASES

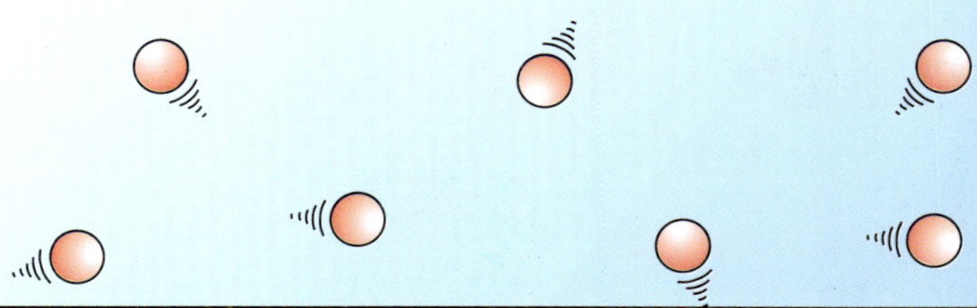

Particles are ...
- FAR APART and ...
- ... there is NO FORCE OF ATTRACTION ...
- ... between the PARTICLES.

Particles can ...
- MOVE AROUND QUICKLY ...
- ... in ANY DIRECTION within their container.

- This is called the **PARTICLE THEORY OF MATTER** and
- ... if we consider how the particles are ARRANGED and MOVE then ...
- ... the PROPERTIES of SOLIDS, LIQUIDS and GASES shown on the previous page, can easily be explained.

1. Draw a diagram to show how the particles are arranged in a) a solid, b) a liquid and c) a gas.
2. Explain how the particles are arranged in a) a solid, b) a liquid and c) a gas.
3. Explain how the particles move in a) a solid, b) a liquid and c) a gas.

EXPANSION, CONTRACTION AND CHANGE OF STATE

As we have seen matter can exist in ONE of three states, SOLID, LIQUID or GAS.
If this matter has ENERGY GIVEN TO IT or TAKEN AWAY then ...

- ... it will either **EXPAND** or **CONTRACT** or ...
- ... if there is a great enough energy transfer a **CHANGE OF STATE** will take place.

EXPANSION AND CONTRACTION

EXPANSION occurs and its TEMPERATURE GOES UP ← ENERGY GIVEN TO IT ← if MATTER has ... → ENERGY TAKEN AWAY → CONTRACTION occurs and its TEMP. GOES DOWN

- The expansion and contraction of matter may CREATE FORCES that are very DAMAGING.
- Railway lines have gaps between sections to prevent buckling during very hot weather.

CHANGE OF STATE - THE PARTICLE THEORY EXPLANATION

Matter may change state ...

- ... by "itself" e.g. EVAPORATION (see page 42) or ...
- ... it may need some help in the fom of ENERGY being GIVEN or TAKEN AWAY.

Let's look at a SOLID which is being SUPPLIED with HEAT ENERGY.

THIS GRAPH IS REVERSIBLE (it would look the same if a gas was being cooled down but the processes would be the opposite way round).

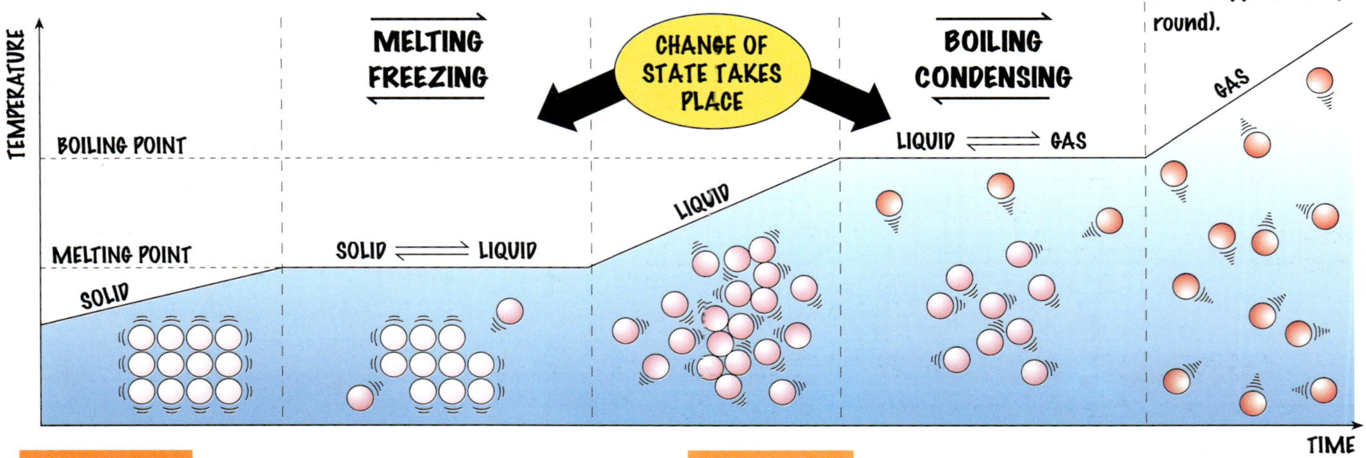

MELTING

<u>When heated</u> ...
- the PARTICLES in a SOLID ...
- ...VIBRATE MORE and MORE.

<u>Eventually</u> ...
- they will have ENOUGH ENERGY ...
- ... to BREAK AWAY from the ...
- ... OTHER PARTICLES in the solid.
- The SOLID has become a LIQUID.

BOILING

<u>When heated</u> ...
- the PARTICLES in a LIQUID ...
- ... MOVE AROUND MORE QUICKLY.

<u>Eventually</u> ...
- they will have ENOUGH ENERGY ...
- ... to ESCAPE from the liquid.
- The LIQUID has become a GAS.

TWO IMPORTANT POINTS

1. When a CHANGE OF STATE takes place ...
   - ... the MASS BEFORE THE CHANGE is **EQUAL** ...
   - ... to the MASS AFTER THE CHANGE.

2. DIFFERENT SUBSTANCES would have graphs ...
   - ... SIMILAR TO ABOVE although they would ...
   - ... CHANGE STATE at DIFFERENT TEMPERATURES.

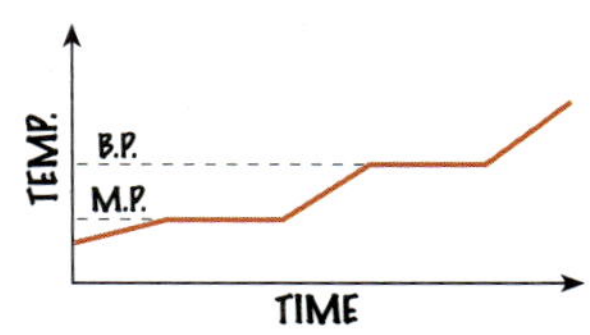

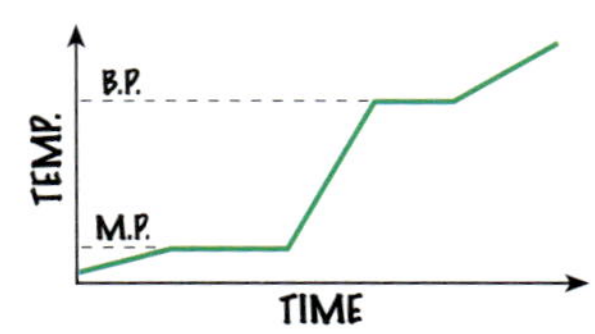

1. Explain what happens if matter has a) energy given to it and b) energy taken away.
2. Give two other examples where the expansion or contraction of matter may create damaging forces.
3. Copy the change of state graph and explain what happens to the particles as they change from a) solid to liquid and b) liquid to gas.

DIFFUSION

If you pass a fish and chip shop when it's nearly lunch time you can't fail to smell the delicious aroma of the food being prepared. The reason this happens is that PARTICLES of GAS given off by the food SPREAD OUT through the AIR. This is **DIFFUSION**.

Diffusion occurs when ...

- TWO DIFFERENT GASES (or LIQUIDS), MIX TOGETHER...
- ... so that the CONCENTRATION OF THE TWO GASES (or LIQUIDS) ...
- ... eventually becomes the SAME EVERY WHERE, because ...
- ... the PARTICLES are CONSTANTLY MOVING. (it doesn't happen in SOLIDS).

Look at these TWO JARS of GAS, ONE containing OXYGEN and the OTHER BROMINE (a brownish gas) ...

... and the PARTICLE THEORY EXPLANATION of what is going on.

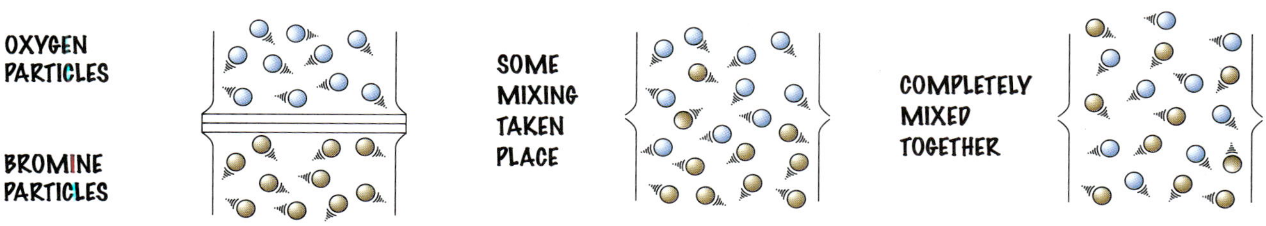

- ALL GAS PARTICLES move around VERY QUICKLY and in ANY DIRECTION.
- There is plenty of SPACE between the particles and so ...
- ... the GASES easily MIX INTO EACH OTHER, until they are evenly spread.
- The same effect can be seen using LIQUIDS but ...
- ... it happens more slowly.

GAS PRESSURE

Look at this BALLOON which has been INFLATED with a GAS.

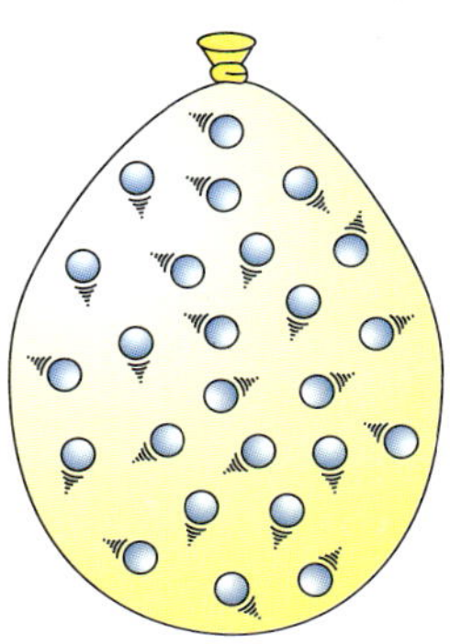

Inside the balloon ...

- GAS PARTICLES are moving around VERY QUICKLY and ...
- ... in ANY DIRECTION.
- MILLIONS of them COLLIDE CONSTANTLY with ...
- ... the INSIDE SURFACE of the balloon.
- This is what we refer to as PRESSURE.

1. What is diffusion? Explain why it doesn't happen in solids? 2. Draw two gas jars, one containing oxygen and the other bromine. Explain using the particle theory what happens if the two gases are allowed to mix.
3. What is gas pressure? Explain using a diagram.

SOIL TYPES

Soil consists of 6 different components ...

• ROCK PARTICLES • MINERAL SALTS • HUMUS • WATER • AIR ... and • LIVING ORGANISMS!

The RELATIVE AMOUNTS of these, give soil its characteristics. There are 3 basic types ...

TYPE	ROCK PARTICLE SIZE	WATER	MINERALS	AIR
SANDY	LARGE. 0.03 - 3mm 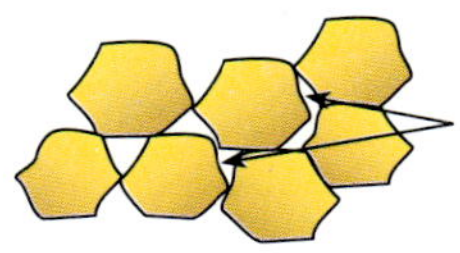 AIR	Good drainage and poor absorption means water is lost quickly. Warms up quickly.	Low mineral content because they are easily leached away.	Lots of air in the spaces between the particles.
CLAY	SMALL. Less than 0.003mm 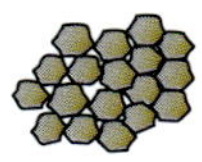 WATER FILLS AIR SPACE	Poor drainage and good absorption means water is held in the soil. Warms up slowly.	High mineral content because they are retained in the soil.	Little air due to water between the particles.
LOAM (or SILT)	INTERMEDIATE. 0.03 - 0.003mm 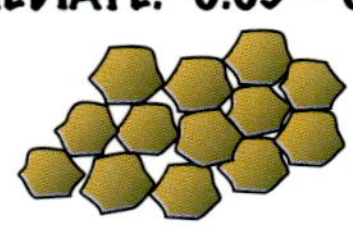	Average drainage. Average absorption of water. Warms up quicker than clay but slower than sandy soil.	Good mineral content as enough minerals are retained.	Has sufficient air to promote good growth.

- HUMUS is the dead organic matter in the soil consisting mainly of LEAF LITTER and MANURE ...
- ... which improves the MOISTURE RETENTION of SANDY SOILS and the AIR AVAILABILITY in CLAY SOILS.
- ORGANISMS help air to circulate and DECOMPOSERS break down dead organic material into INORGANIC MATERIAL.
- The ROOTS of GREEN PLANTS help to bind the soil together preventing erosion.

ROCK TYPES

There are 3 basic types of rock ...

• SEDIMENTARY • METAMORPHIC • IGNEOUS

TYPE	EXAMPLES	CHARACTERISTICS
SEDIMENTARY	• SANDSTONE • LIMESTONE	GRAINY AND CRUMBLY. THEY MAY CONTAIN FOSSILS.
METAMORPHIC	• SLATE • MARBLE	SMALL CRYSTALS IN LAYERS (or bands). HARD AND SMOOTH.
IGNEOUS	• BASALT • GRANITE	SMALL CRYSTALS DUE TO FAST COOLING. HARD ROCKS. LARGE CRYSTALS DUE TO SLOW COOLING. HARD ROCKS.

You really do need to see these rocks in order to understand these descriptions. (Also see page 35.)
Really look hard with a hand lens when your teacher gives you the opportunity.

1. What are the six different components of soil?
2. Explain how sandy, clay and loam soils differ in a) rock particle size, b) drainage of water, c) mineral content and d) air content.
3. What are the three different types of rock? Give two examples of each.

THE ROCK CYCLE

- The ROCK CYCLE is an ongoing CYCLE OF EVENTS where ROCKS at the EARTH'S SURFACE are continually being BROKEN UP, REFORMED and CHANGED.

WEATHERING OF ROCKS

- This is the name of the process whereby rocks at the surface get broken up. Weathering is caused by ...

1. Effect of the sun

- During the DAY the rocks are WARMED UP and EXPAND while ...
- ... at NIGHT they COOL DOWN and CONTRACT (shrink).
- Over many years this can lead to the ROCKS CRACKING and eventually BREAKING UP INTO SMALLER PIECES.

2. Effect of freezing water

- Any WATER which gets into CRACKS in ROCKS will EXPAND when it FREEZES.
- Over many years this can lead to the CRACKS getting BIGGER and BIGGER ...
- ... which eventually causes the rock to BREAK UP INTO SMALLER PIECES.

THE ROCK CYCLE

This only involves THREE different kinds of rock ...
... SEDIMENTARY, METAMORPHIC and IGNEOUS, which are involved in a continuous slow UPLIFT and EROSION.

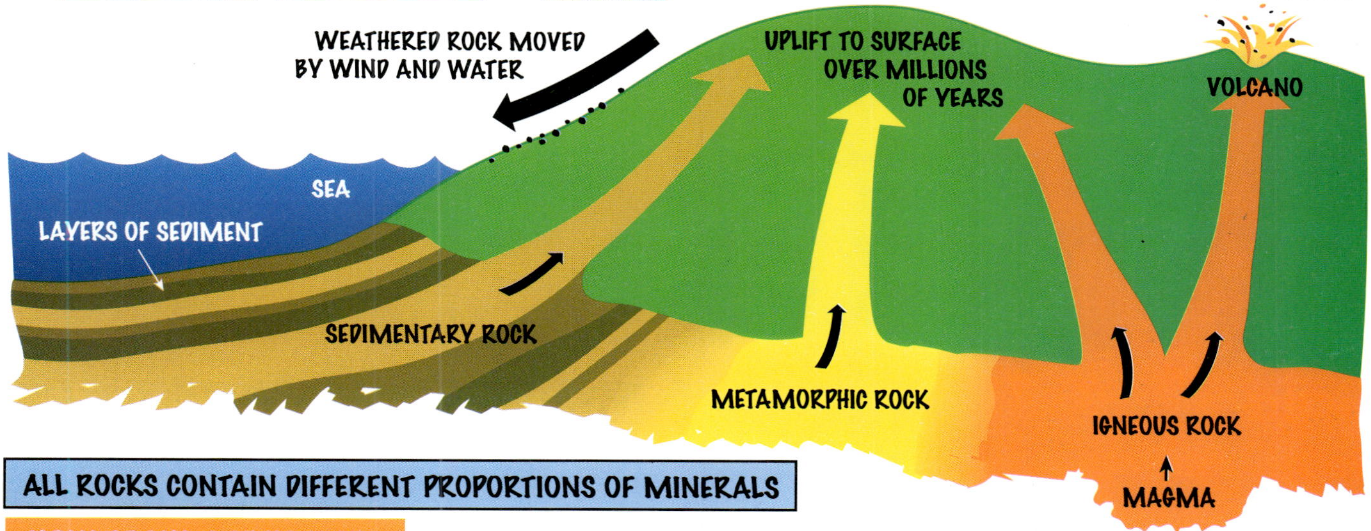

ALL ROCKS CONTAIN DIFFERENT PROPORTIONS OF MINERALS

HOW ROCKS ARE FORMED

TYPE	HOW THEY ARE FORMED	EXAMPLES
SEDIMENTARY	• Formed from LAYERS of SEDIMENT. (small pieces of weathered rock) ... • ... which are SQUEEZED ... • ... to become CEMENTED TOGETHER.	SANDSTONE LIMESTONE
METAMORPHIC	• Formed from SEDIMENTARY ROCKS ... • ... which have been PUSHED DEEP UNDERGROUND ... • ... where they are COMPRESSED and HEATED ... • ... changing the way they look.	SLATE (from mudstone) MARBLE (from limestone)
IGNEOUS	• Formed from LIQUID ROCK called MAGMA ... • ... which comes up from the MANTLE ... • ... and COOLS DOWN either ... • ... ABOVE or WITHIN the earth's crust.	BASALT (expelled from volcanos) GRANITE (magma cooled inside earth's crust)

1. What are the two ways that rocks can be weathered? Explain using diagrams.
2. Draw the rock cycle and explain how sedimentary, metamorphic and igneous rocks are formed.

ELEMENTS

ELEMENTS, ATOMS AND PROTONS

An element is a pure substance in which all of the atoms are identical, i.e. they all contain the same number of PROTONS.

For instance,

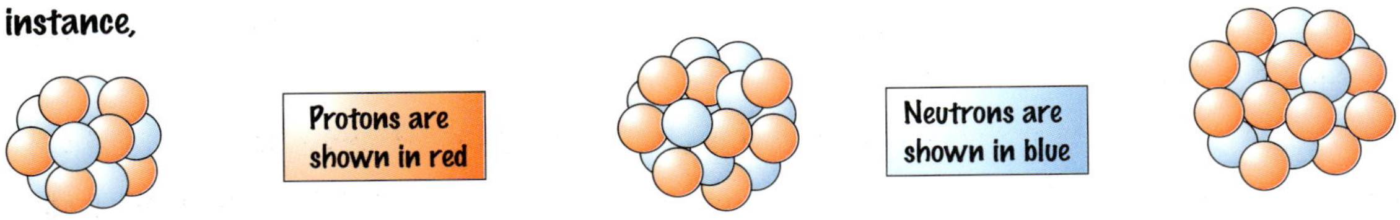

ALL CARBON atoms contain 6 PROTONS

ALL OXYGEN atoms contain 8 PROTONS

ALL SODIUM atoms contain 11 PROTONS

- The other particles in the atom are NEUTRONS (and ELECTRONS which "whizz" round the whole lot) but it is only the number of PROTONS which decide which element the atom is.

THE PERIODIC TABLE

This table is a way of classifying all the elements.

- The elements are arranged IN ORDER OF INCREASING NUMBER of PROTONS (i.e. PROTON NUMBER) ...
- ... into EIGHT GROUPS which have SIMILAR PROPERTIES.
- EACH ELEMENT HAS ITS OWN SYMBOL ...

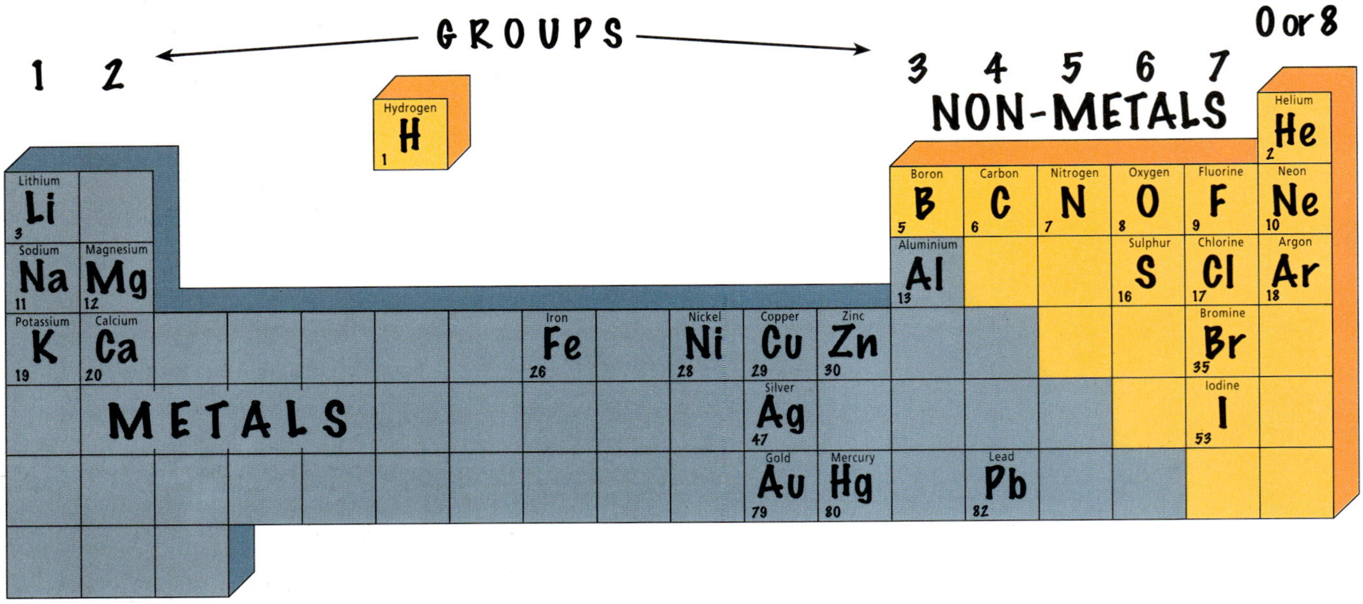

This periodic table contains only those elements which you need to know, and contains their symbol and proton no.

COMPARING METALS AND NON-METALS

METALS	NON-METALS
• All are SHINY SOLIDS at room temperature (except Mercury which is a liquid.) • GOOD CONDUCTORS of heat and electricity when solid or liquid. • A FEW ARE MAGNETIC.	• Half of them are GASES at room temperature. • POOR CONDUCTORS of heat and electricity when solid or liquid. • VARY WIDELY IN THEIR PHYSICAL PROPERTIES.

1. What is an element?
2. What is the periodic table? Draw out the periodic table above, making sure you label the metals and the non-metals.
3. What are the main differences between metals and non-metals?

A DEFINITION OF A COMPOUND

A COMPOUND is a SUBSTANCE which is made up of ...

- ... the ATOMS of TWO or MORE ELEMENTS which have been JOINED TOGETHER ...
- ... because a CHEMICAL REACTION has taken place.
- When atoms join together they form MOLECULES, and are chemically combined and difficult to separate.

Take a look at these examples ...

No.1 SODIUM CHLORIDE

This compound is formed from a METAL, SODIUM and a GAS, CHLORINE.

SODIUM + CHLORINE —CHEMICAL REACTION TAKES PLACE→ SODIUM CHLORIDE, NaCl

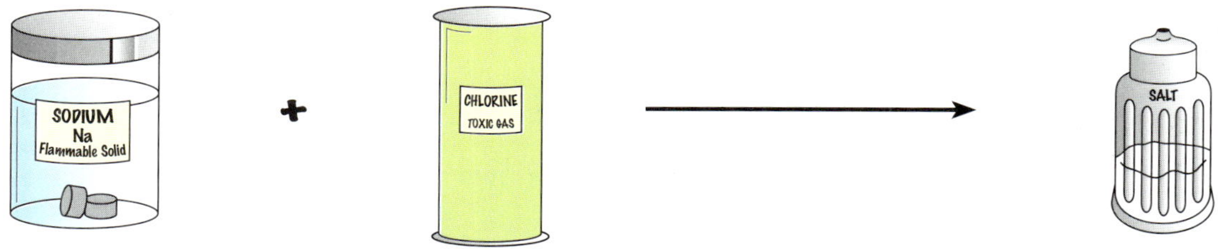

... and if we think of the atoms involved ...

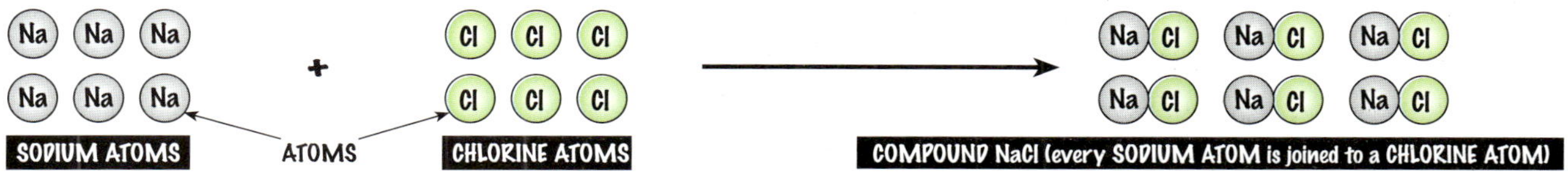

No.2 WATER

This COMPOUND is formed from TWO GASES, HYDROGEN and OXYGEN (both colourless).

HYDROGEN + OXYGEN —CHEMICAL REACTION TAKES PLACE→ WATER, H_2O

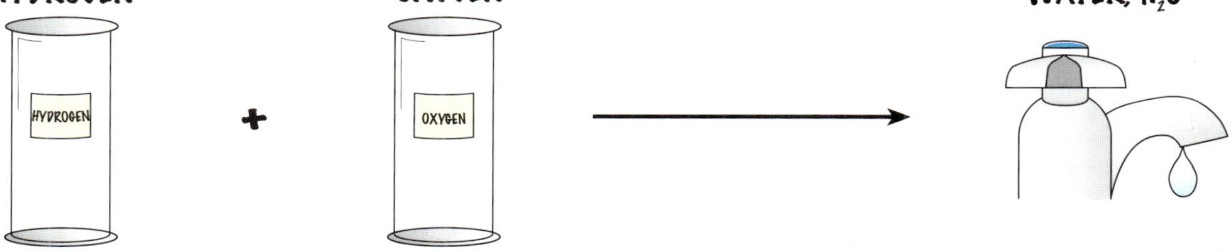

... and if we think of the atoms involved ...

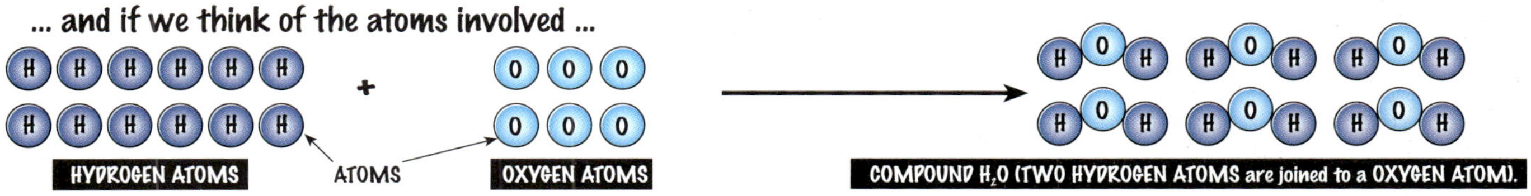

No.3 CARBON DIOXIDE

This COMPOUND is formed from a NON-METAL, CARBON and a GAS OXYGEN.

CARBON + OXYGEN —CHEMICAL REACTION TAKES PLACE→ CARBON DIOXIDE, CO_2

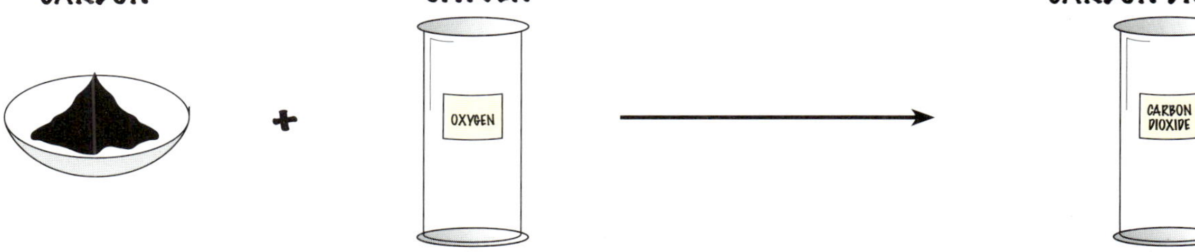

... and if we think of the atoms involved ...

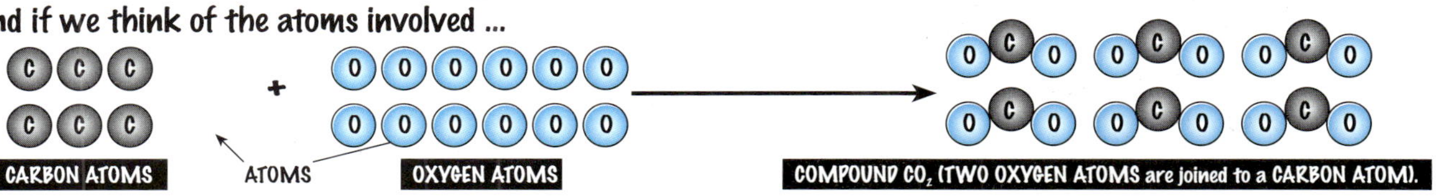

1. What is a compound?
2. Explain using atoms how the following compounds are formed: a) Sodium Chloride, NaCl b) Carbon Dioxide, CO_2 and c) Magnesium Oxide, MgO.
3. Name THREE other examples of compounds which are not stated above.

A DEFINITION OF A MIXTURE

A mixture is a SUBSTANCE which is made up of the ATOMS of TWO or MORE ELEMENTS ...
- ... or COMPOUNDS which have NOT been JOINED TOGETHER IN A CHEMICAL REACTION ...
- ... and are EASY TO SEPARATE.

Take a look at these examples ...

No. 1 AIR

- Air is a MIXTURE OF GASES made up of ...
- ... mainly NITROGEN and OXYGEN (TWO ELEMENTS) and ...
- ... small amounts of CARBON DIOXIDE (a COMPOUND).
- The OXYGEN atoms "PAIR-UP" to form MOLECULES, as do the NITROGEN atoms.

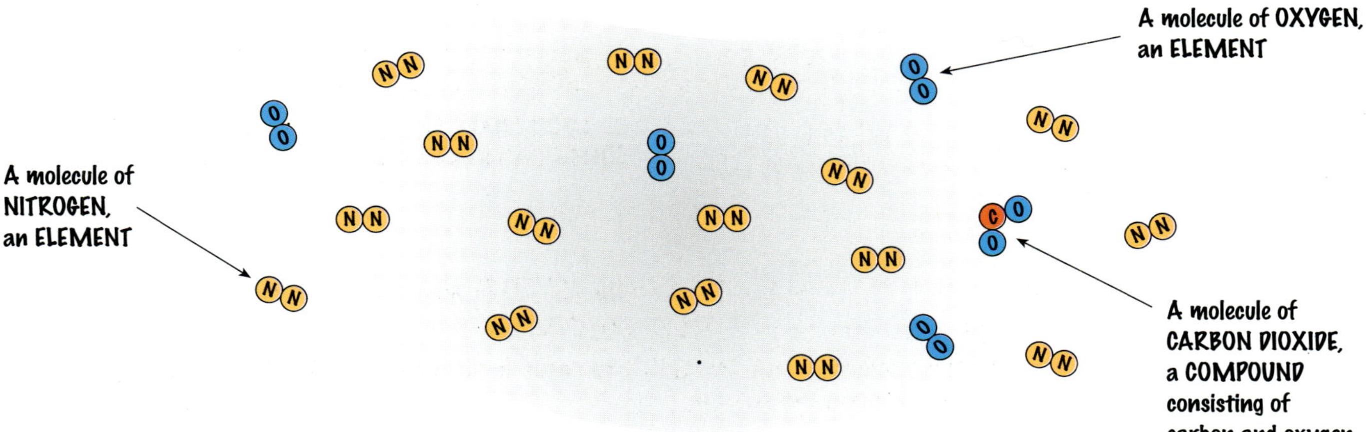

No. 2 SEA WATER

- SEA WATER is a MIXTURE of SOLIDS, LIQUIDS and GASES made up mainly from ...
- ... WATER and SALT (which is dissolved in the water) ...
- ... with very small amounts of OTHER COMPOUNDS.

This PIE CHART gives you some idea of the composition of SEA WATER.

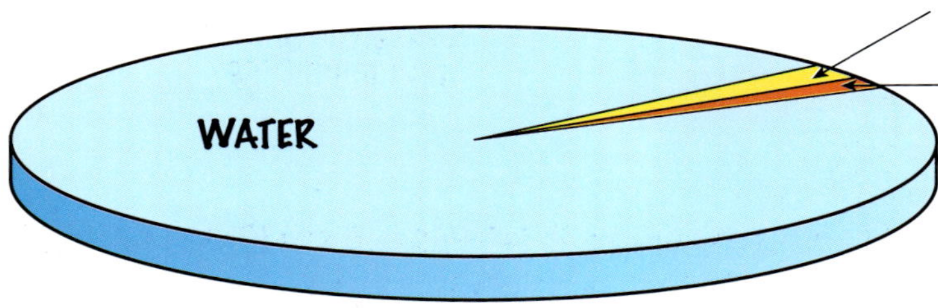

OTHER EXAMPLES

MILK

- Liquid fat and water

'FIZZY' POP

- Water, carbon dioxide and others

CRUDE OIL

- Petrol, diesel, bitumen and others

1. What is a mixture? In what way is a mixture different to a compound?
2. Explain why a) air and b) sea water are mixtures?
3. Name 3 other examples (not stated above) of mixtures.

SOLUTIONS - ANOTHER TYPE OF MIXTURE

FACTORS AFFECTING SOLUBILITY

The SOLUBILITY of a SOLUTE in a SOLVENT at a particular TEMPERATURE is ...
... a measure of how much substance will dissolve in the solvent at that temperature.
In the first example below, COFFEE is the SOLUTE and WATER is the SOLVENT.
Together they form a SOLUTION.

1. TEMPERATURE OF THE SOLVENT

Very simply ...
- the HOTTER the LIQUID (SOLVENT) ...
- ... the QUICKER the SOLID (SOLUTE) DISSOLVES (providing it does dissolve in the first place).

Let's consider adding instant coffee to water at different temperatures.

ALL THESE BEAKERS HAVE THE SAME AMOUNT (MASS) OF COFFEE ADDED TO EQUAL VOLUMES OF WATER.

A LITTLE BIT OF COFFEE HAS DISSOLVED

ABOUT HALF THE COFFEE HAS DISSOLVED.

ALL THE COFFEE HAS DISSOLVED.

2. MASS AND TYPE OF SOLUTE ADDED

Very simply ...
- There is a LIMIT to the MASS of SOLID (SOLUTE) which can dissolve ...
- ... in a particular amount of LIQUID (SOLVENT).
- The amount needed for SATURATION to occur is different for different solutes.
  i.e. they have different SOLUBILITIES.

Again let's consider adding instant coffee to water ...

ALL THE COFFEE HAS DISSOLVED.

AGAIN THE COFFEE HAS DISSOLVED.

NONE WILL DISSOLVE - THE COFFEE ADDED SINKS TO THE BOTTOM. THE SOLUTION IS SATURATED.

3. TYPE OF SOLVENT USED

Very simply ...
- A SOLID (SOLUTE) which DISSOLVES in ONE LIQUID (SOLVENT) ...
- ... may NOT DISSOLVE in ANOTHER LIQUID .

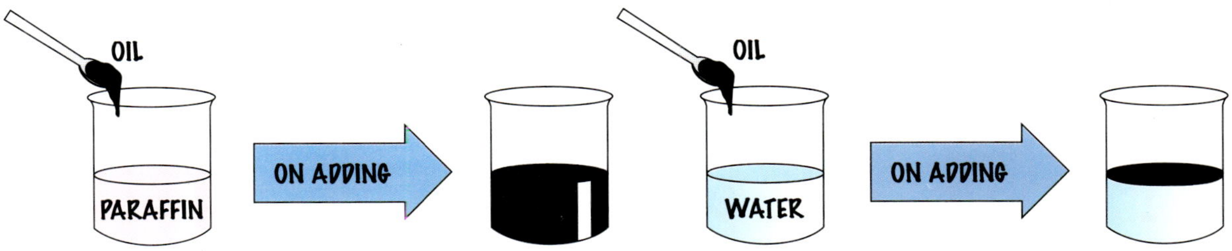

ALL THE OIL HAS DISSOLVED.

THE OIL JUSTS FLOATS ON THE WATER.

This is why car mechanics use Paraffin rather than water to remove oil.

1. Write definitions of a) a solute, b) a solvent and c) a solution in your own words.
2. Explain using diagrams how the following factors affect the solubility of a solute: a) temperature of the solvent b) mass and type of solute added and c) type of solvent used.

The substances which make up a mixture can be SEPARATED from EACH OTHER if necessary.
Here are FIVE methods which cover most possibilities.

SIEVING

Used to separate ...
- SOLID PARTICLES which are DIFFERENT IN SIZE.
- e.g. SOIL is made up of many SOLID PARTICLES of DIFFERENT SIZES.

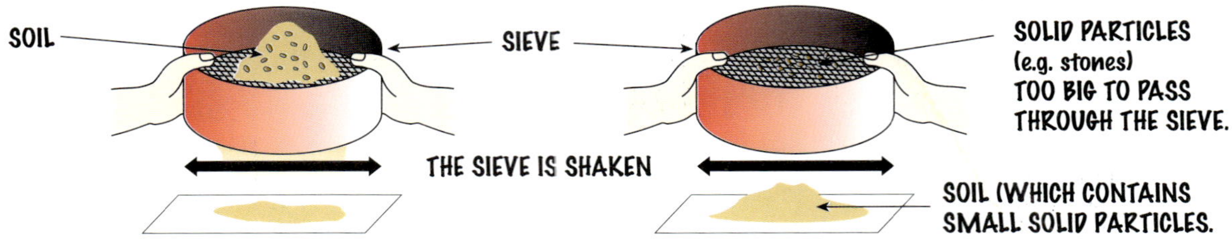

FILTRATION

Used to separate ...
- an INSOLUBLE SOLID FROM A LIQUID.
- e.g. a MIXTURE of SAND and WATER, or CHALK and WATER.

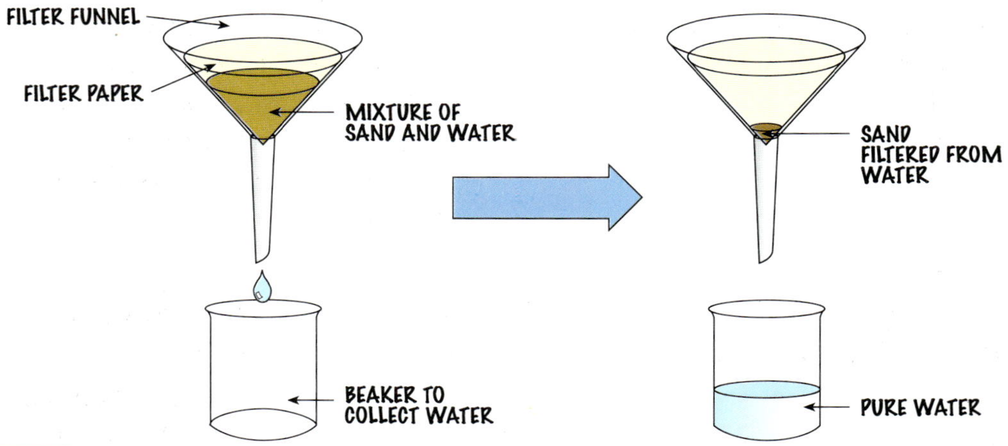

EVAPORATION

Used to separate ...
- a SOLUBLE SOLID FROM A LIQUID when ...
- ... we want to COLLECT the SOLID.
- e.g. a MIXTURE of SALT and WATER, or SUGAR and WATER.

- BOIL THE SOLUTION AND THE WATER EVAPORATES leaving SALT BEHIND usually as SMALL CRYSTALS, however ...
- ... if you let it EVAPORATE SLOWLY, you'll get BIG SALT CRYSTALS.

The above TWO methods can be used to SEPARATE a MIXTURE of TWO SOLIDS, ONE of which is SOLUBLE ...
- ... e.g. a MIXTURE of SALT and SAND where you ...
- ... ADD THE MIXTURE to WATER and STIR. THE SALT DISSOLVES while THE SAND SINKS TO THE BOTTOM.
- The whole lot is then filtered to separate the sand from the solution of salt and water ...
- ... which is then evaporated to dryness to leave behind the salt.

1. Draw diagrams to show how: a) sieving b) filtration and c) evaporation can be used to separate the substances which make up a mixture.
2. Explain using diagrams how a mixture of salt and sand can be separated.

CHROMATOGRAPHY

This is used to separate ...

- SMALL AMOUNTS of TWO or MORE SOLIDS ...
- ... all of which are SOLUBLE in a particular LIQUID (SOLVENT).
- e.g. separation of the PIGMENTS in COLOURED INKS.

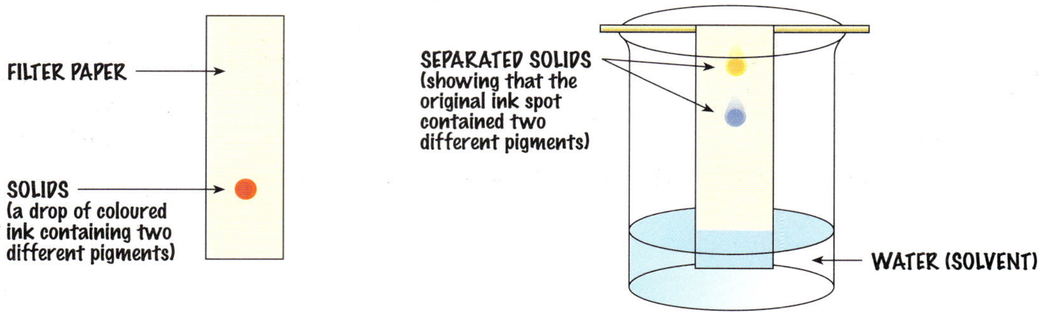

- DISSOLVE THE MIXTURE OF SOLIDS ...
- ... in a suitable SOLVENT (WATER).
- Put a DROP of SOLUTION on the FILTER PAPER.
- The SOLVENT EVAPORATES to ...
- ... leave the SOLIDS BEHIND.
- The sample being investigated must remain above the water level, which covers the bottom cm. of the filter paper.
- As the solvent rises up the paper ...
- ... the solids dissolve in the solvent ...
- ... and are carried up the paper.
- The MORE SOLUBLE SOLIDS TRAVEL FURTHER UP THE PAPER.

DISTILLATION

This is used to separate ...

- ... a LIQUID from SOLIDS which are DISSOLVED IN IT, when we want to collect the liquid
- e.g. distillation of SEAWATER (SALT WATER SOLUTION) to produce pure water.

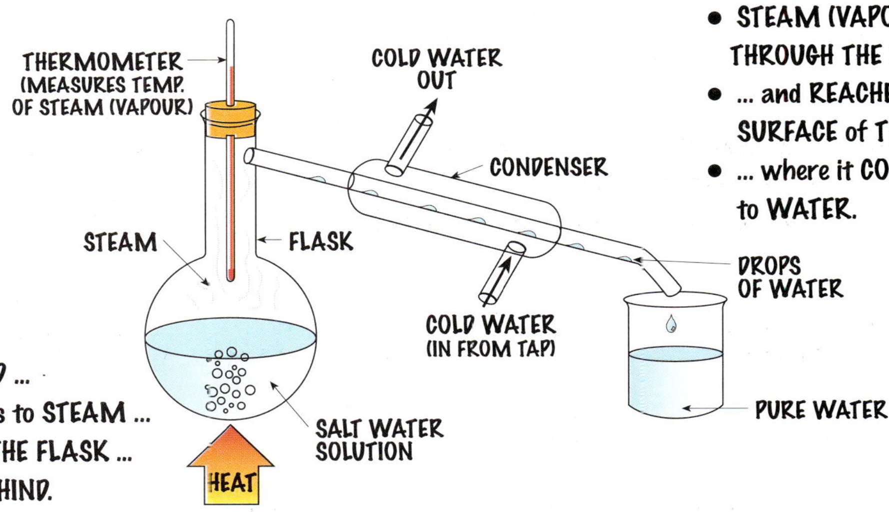

- STEAM (VAPOUR) PASSES THROUGH THE TUBING ...
- ... and REACHES THE COLD SURFACE of THE CONDENSER ...
- ... where it CONDENSES back to WATER.
- THE SALT WATER SOLUTION IS BOILED ...
- ... and WATER turns to STEAM ...
- ... which RISES UP THE FLASK ...
- ... LEAVING SALT BEHIND.

The above methods can also be used to separate ...

- ... a MIXTURE of TWO LIQUIDS which have DIFFERENT BOILING POINTS.
- e.g. a mixture of ALCOHOL and WATER.
- The ALCOHOL BOILS FIRST (alcohol boils at about 78°C) and ...
- ... its VAPOUR is CONDENSED BACK INTO PURE ALCOHOL.
- The WATER is LEFT BEHIND in the FLASK.

1. Draw diagrams to show how: a) chromatography and b) distillation can be used to separate the substances which make up a mixture.
2. Explain using diagrams how a mixture of alcohol and water can be separated.

In chemistry there are two kinds of change: PHYSICAL and CHEMICAL.

1. PHYSICAL CHANGE

- This is when NO NEW MATERIAL IS MADE although ...
- ... the material may CHANGE in APPEARANCE.
- It is QUITE EASY to RETURN to the MATERIAL WE STARTED WITH and so ...
- ... the CHANGE is REVERSIBLE. e.g. change of state, formation of solution (see page 39).

... while on a LARGER SCALE there is the WATER CYCLE.

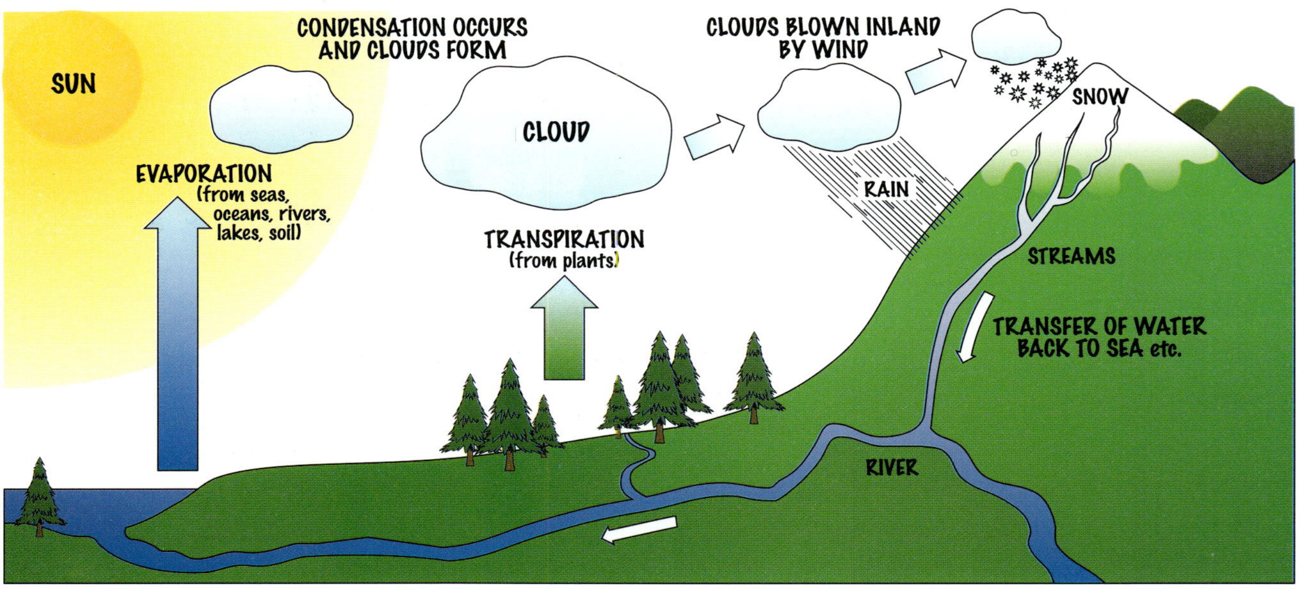

- ENERGY from the SUN causes WATER VAPOUR TO RISE by ... EVAPORATION and TRANSPIRATION.
- As the WATER VAPOUR RISES HIGHER AND HIGHER ... it COOLS and CONDENSATION occurs ...
- ... forming DROPLETS OF WATER ... which collect together to form CLOUDS.
- RAIN and possibly SLEET or SNOW falls when the droplets are big enough and the CYCLE BEGINS AGAIN.

2. CHEMICAL CHANGE

- This is when A NEW MATERIAL IS MADE in a CHEMICAL REACTION.
- The material DOES CHANGE in APPEARANCE.
- It is VERY DIFFICULT to RETURN to the MATERIAL WE STARTED WITH and so ...
- ... the CHANGE is NOT REVERSIBLE, under normal conditions.

HEATING up DOUGH gives us BREAD.

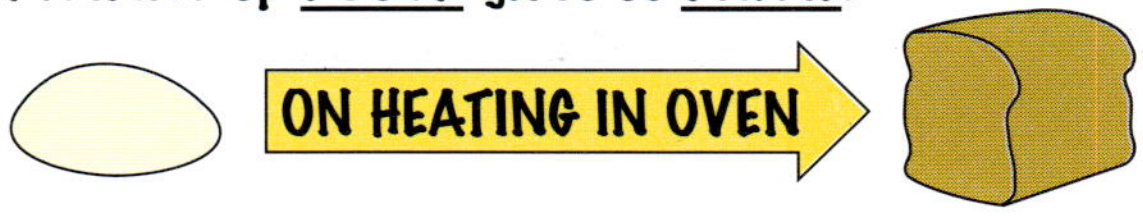

HEATING up CLAY gives us BRICK.

You will meet many more examples of these CHEMICAL REACTIONS on the following pages ...

1. What is a physical change? Give TWO examples.
2. Draw a fully labelled diagram of the water cycle and explain how it works.
3. What is a chemical change? Give TWO examples.

WHAT IS A CHEMICAL REACTION?

Let's consider what happens when a MIXTURE of IRON and SULPHUR is HEATED ...

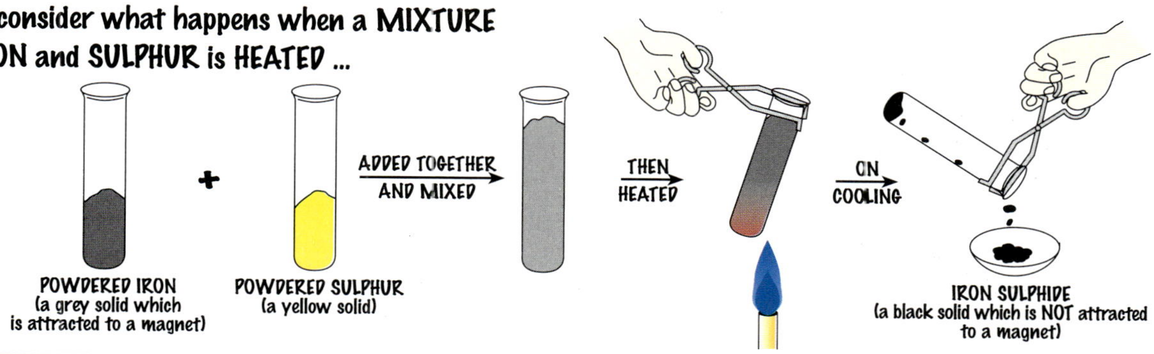

A **CHEMICAL REACTION** has taken place because, we STARTED OFF with TWO ELEMENTS, IRON and SULPHUR and ENDED UP with a COMPOUND, IRON SULPHIDE which LOOKS and BEHAVES DIFFERENTLY.

This chemical reaction can be written as a WORD EQUATION ...

Iron + Sulphur ⟶ Iron Sulphide

- The IRON and SULPHUR are called the REACTANTS while ...
- ... the IRON SULPHIDE is called the PRODUCT.

N.B. IN ALL CHEMICAL REACTIONS, THE MASS AT THE END OF THE REACTION IS EQUAL TO THE MASS WE STARTED OFF WITH BEFORE THE REACTION

THERMAL DECOMPOSITION

This is a chemical reaction where a COMPOUND is BROKEN DOWN into SIMPLER SUBSTANCES when it is HEATED (compare with above).

- An example is the THERMAL DECOMPOSITION of SILVER OXIDE ...

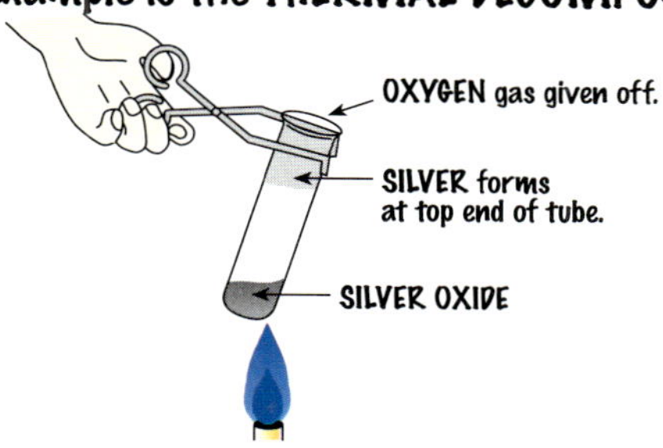

... and the WORD EQUATION for the chemical reaction that has taken place is ...

Silver oxide ⟶ Silver + Oxygen

PRODUCTION OF METALS

- The thermal decomposition of SILVER OXIDE is a simple way of producing SILVER, a metal ... ... from SILVER OXIDE by REMOVING THE OXYGEN.
- Many METALS exist naturally in the ground as an OXIDE and ... ... to get the METAL ON IT'S OWN THE OXYGEN MUST BE REMOVED.
- This is known as REDUCTION.

Example 1 - PRODUCTION OF IRON

IRON exists as IRON OXIDE. The OXYGEN IS REMOVED BY HEATING THE IRON OXIDE with CARBON in a BLAST FURNACE.

Iron oxide + Carbon ⟶ Iron + Carbon dioxide

Example 2 - PRODUCTION OF ALUMINIUM

ALUMINIUM exists as ALUMINIUM OXIDE, however the OXYGEN CANNOT be removed by using heat. This time we have to use an ELECTRIC CURRENT in a process called ELECTROLYSIS.

Aluminium oxide ⟶ Aluminium + Oxygen

1. What is a chemical reaction?
2. What is thermal decomposition?
3. What is reduction? Explain how Iron and Aluminium are produced.

OXIDATION REACTIONS

These are very common reactions where a SUBSTANCE REACTS WITH OXYGEN.
Oxidation reactions can be USEFUL but they are also proving to be ENVIRONMENTALLY DAMAGING

BURNING

ALL FUELS (e.g. WOOD, COAL, WAX) BURN in OXYGEN producing ...

- ... HEAT (and LIGHT) and
- ... CARBON DIOXIDE and WATER. These are the WASTE PRODUCTS.

e.g. NATURAL GAS is made up mainly of METHANE ...

Methane + Oxygen ⟶ Carbon dioxide + Water + HEAT

... while this simple experiment shows that if there is NOT ENOUGH OXYGEN AVAILABLE ...
... then the FUEL is INCOMPLETELY BURNED.

The HEAT PRODUCED when FUELS are BURNED in controlled reactions is used ...

- ... to PROVIDE WARMTH and to COOK WITH and also ...
- ... in the GENERATION OF ELECTRICITY in POWER STATIONS.

ENVIRONMENTAL PROBLEMS WITH BURNING FUELS

As we have seen, BURNING a FUEL produces HEAT but ...

- ... it also produces CARBON DIOXIDE.
- CARBON DIOXIDE is one of the GREENHOUSE GASES responsible for GLOBAL WARMING.
- The INCREASED BURNING of FOSSIL FUELS because of the INDUSTRIAL REVOLUTION ...
- ... has caused an INCREASED RELEASE of CARBON DIOXIDE into the ATMOSPHERE ...
- ... which is NOW proving to be ENVIRONMENTALLY DAMAGING.

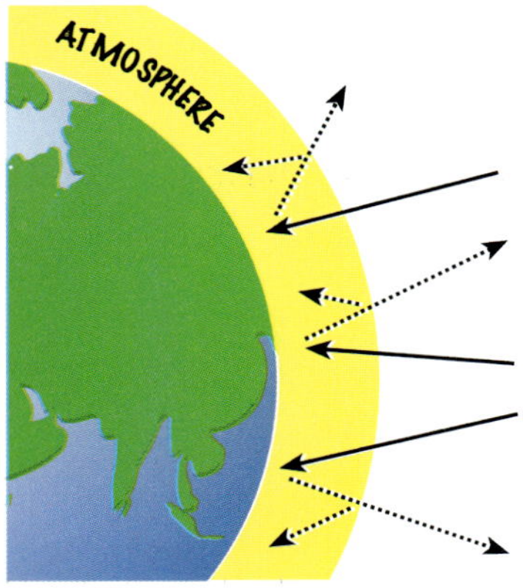

- Light from the SUN reaches the EARTH ...
- ... and passes through the ATMOSPHERE.
- This WARMS up the earth which then sends this heat energy ...
- ... back into SPACE.

However

- CARBON DIOXIDE helps to trap some of this energy ...
- ... which helps to keep the earth WARM.
- TOO MUCH CARBON DIOXIDE however, leads to too much heat being retained.
- This is GLOBAL WARMING.

1. What is an oxidation reaction?
2. Why is burning an oxidation reaction? Write a word equation for the burning of methane.
3. What is global warming? Explain using a diagram.

RUSTING OF IRON (OR STEEL)

Let's look at these THREE test tubes which have been set up and left to stand for a few days.

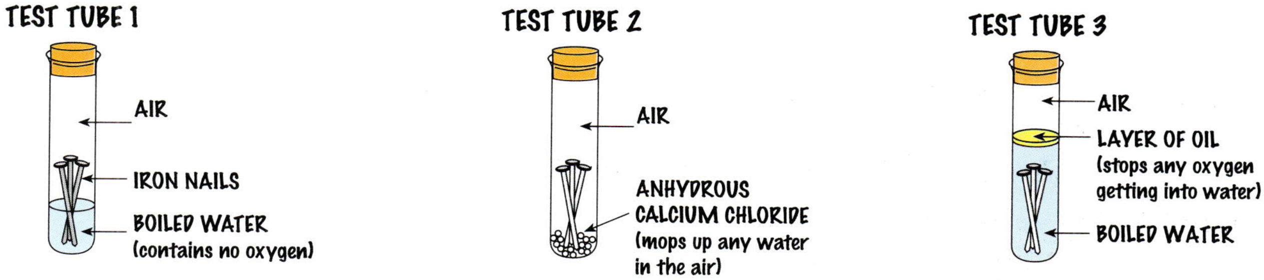

TEST TUBE	IS OXYGEN PRESENT?	IS WATER PRESENT?	HAS RUSTING OCCURED?
1	YES	YES	YES
2	YES	NO	NO
3	NO	YES	NO

From the results we can see that TWO things are necessary for RUSTING TO OCCUR ...
... **OXYGEN** and ... **WATER** (salty water causes even faster rusting).

Iron + Oxygen ⟶ Iron Oxide

and then ... Iron Oxide + Water ⟶ Hydrated Iron Oxide (BROWN CRUMBLY RUST).

Rusting can prove to be VERY EXPENSIVE as it WEAKENS the metal and REDUCES IT'S WORKING LIFE. It needs to be stopped.

PREVENTION OF RUSTING

- The simplest way is to COAT THE SURFACE OF THE METAL WITH A PROTECTIVE LAYER as ...
- ... this STOPS any CONTACT with AIR (OXYGEN) or WATER.
- The most common protective layers are ...
- ... **PAINT** ...
- ... **OIL or GREASE** ...
- ... **PLASTIC** ...
- ... **TIN or CHROMIUM PLATING.**

  e.g. Cars are painted!!

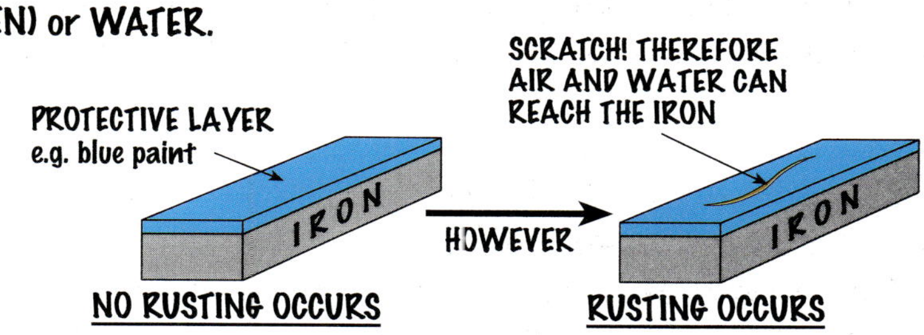

FOOD SPOILAGE

- Certain foods contain CHEMICALS ...
- ... which REACT with the OXYGEN in the AIR ...
- ... forming NEW CHEMICALS which are ...
- ... rather nasty as they affect both the ...
- ... APPEARANCE and FLAVOUR of the food.

- This OXIDATION of food can be prevented by ...
- ... adding **ANTI-OXIDANTS** to the food or ...
- ... by **VACUUM PACKING** the food where ...
- ... ALL THE AIR has been REMOVED.

1. Explain using diagrams how you would perform a simple experiment to show the conditions needed for the rusting of Iron.
2. Name THREE ways of preventing rusting?
3. Why does food become spoiled? Explain how this can be prevented.

THE REACTIVITY SERIES

Some METALS willingly COMBINE with OTHER ELEMENTS to form new COMPOUNDS. By observing how metals REACT with OXYGEN (AIR), WATER and DILUTE ACID we can place them in order of how vigorously they react. We call this list the REACTIVITY SERIES and this is it ...

	ELEMENT	REACTION WITH OXYGEN (AIR)	REACTION WITH WATER	REACTION WITH DILUTE ACID
VERY REACTIVE	POTASSIUM	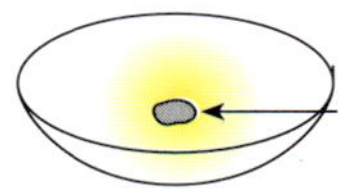 SODIUM BURNS BRIGHTLY WHEN HEATED TO FORM OXIDE	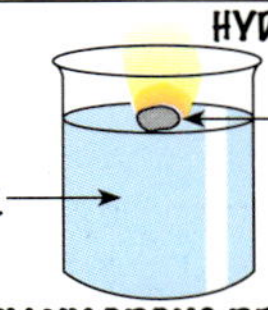 HYDROGEN GAS, SODIUM, WATER VERY VIGOROUS REACTION IN COLD WATER FORMS HYDROXIDE	 VIOLENT REACTION AND VERY DANGEROUS
VERY REACTIVE	SODIUM			
VERY REACTIVE	CALCIUM	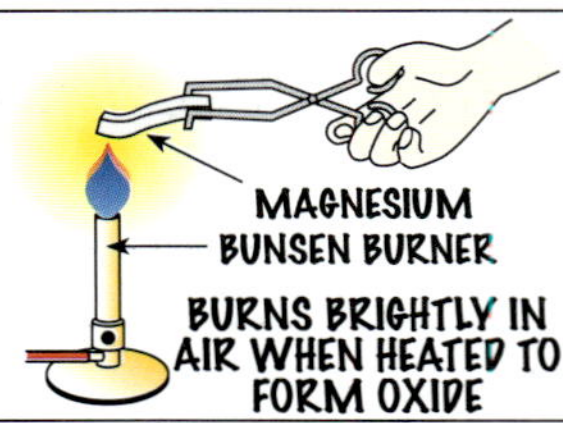 MAGNESIUM, BUNSEN BURNER BURNS BRIGHTLY IN AIR WHEN HEATED TO FORM OXIDE	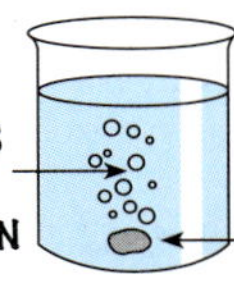 BUBBLES OF HYDROGEN, CALCIUM SLOW REACTION IN COLD WATER TO FORM HYDROXIDE	
QUITE REACTIVE	MAGNESIUM			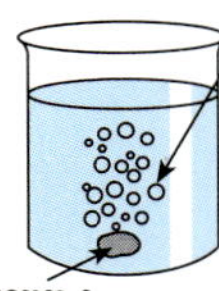 HYDROGEN GAS, MAGNESIUM REASONABLE REACTION WHICH DECREASES AS WE GO DOWN 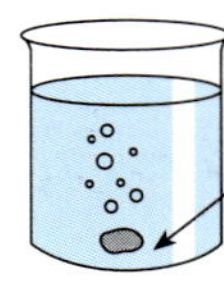 IRON
QUITE REACTIVE	ALUMINIUM	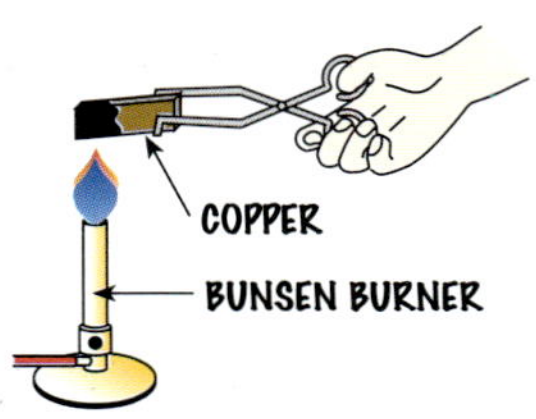 COPPER, BUNSEN BURNER REACT SLOWLY WHEN HEATED TO FORM OXIDE	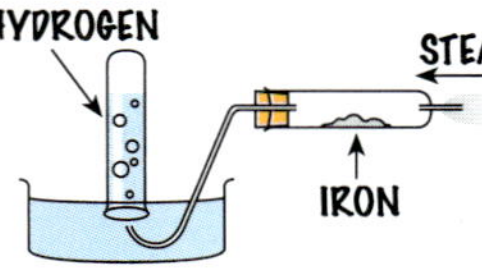 HYDROGEN, STEAM, IRON REACTS WITH STEAM BUT NOT WATER TO FORM OXIDE	
QUITE REACTIVE	ZINC			
NOT SO REACTIVE	IRON			
NOT SO REACTIVE	TIN			
NOT SO REACTIVE	LEAD		 COPPER NO REACTION WITH WATER OR STEAM	
	HYDROGEN			
NOT SO REACTIVE	COPPER			 GOLD NO REACTION
NOT REACTIVE AT ALL	SILVER	 SILVER, BUNSEN BURNER NO REACTION		
NOT REACTIVE AT ALL	GOLD			

INCREASING REACTIVITY (upwards)

- Metals react with acids to form various salts (see page 49).

1. What is the reactivity series?
2. Why is gold found in pure form?
3. Why have lead and copper traditionally been used for pipes?

A DISPLACEMENT REACTION is one in which a MORE REACTIVE metal displaces a LESS REACTIVE metal from a compound in a chemical reaction.

There's just one "incredibly important rule" to remember!

IF THE PURE METAL IS HIGHER IN THE REACTIVITY SERIES THAN THE METAL IN THE COMPOUND, THEN DISPLACEMENT WILL HAPPEN.

Let's consider what happens when an IRON NAIL is put into a beaker of COPPER SULPHATE SOLUTION.

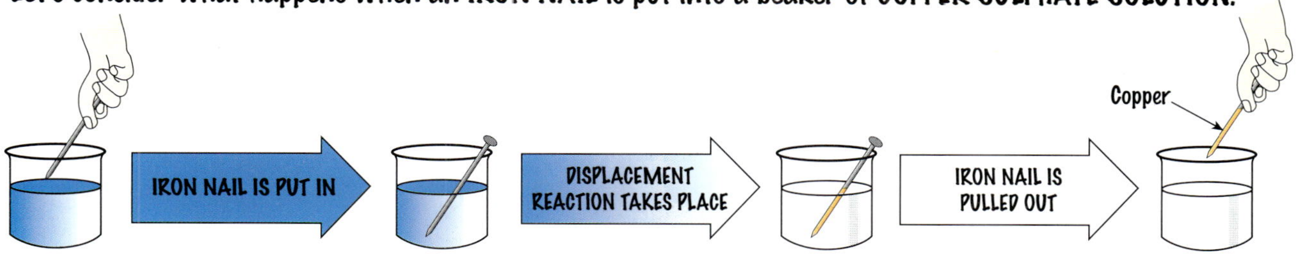

If we look at the POSITIONS of IRON and COPPER in the REACTIVITY SERIES, then what's gone on above can easily be explained

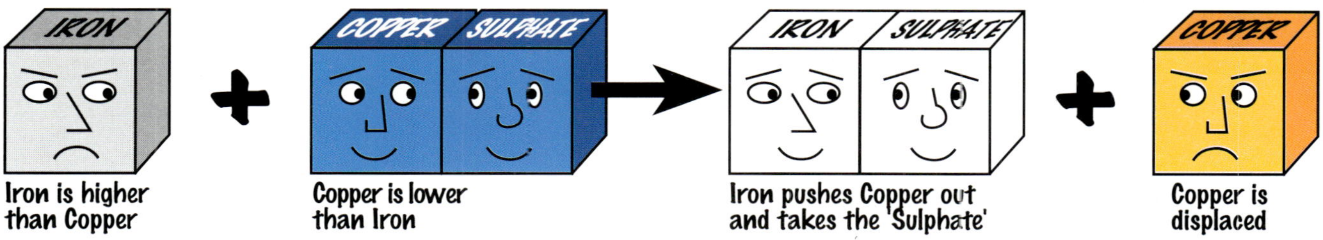

This is why an iron nail becomes coated with Copper when it's put in Copper Sulphate Solution, and why the blue solution becomes clear Iron Sulphate solution.

SOME MORE EXAMPLES OF DISPLACEMENT

Example No. 1

ZINC + COPPER SULPHATE SOLUTION

Remember the "Rule". Which is HIGHER in the Reactivity series?

ZINC + COPPER SULPHATE ⟶ ZINC SULPHATE + COPPER

Yes! Zinc is higher so it displaces the copper forming Zinc Sulphate.

Example No. 2

COPPER + LEAD NITRATE SOLUTION

Remember the "Rule". Which is HIGHER in the Reactivity series?

COPPER + LEAD NITRATE ⟶ LEAD NITRATE + COPPER

No! Copper is lower in the series than Lead so no reaction takes place.

SUMMING UP

- Look at the Reactivity Series ...
- ... If the pure metal is higher than the metal in the metal compound ...
- ... then simply swop the metals around!!
- If it isn't there's no reaction.

1. Write out the "incredibly important rule" above.
2. Complete the following equations using the rule: a) Lead + Copper Chloride ⟶ b) Silver + Copper Chloride ⟶ c) Magnesium + Iron Oxide ⟶ d) Aluminium + Copper Sulphate ⟶ e) Zinc + Lead Nitrate ⟶

INDICATORS

These are really useful dyes which CHANGE COLOUR ...

- ... depending on whether they're in ACIDIC or ALKALINE solutions.
- Some are just simple substances such as LITMUS which changes from RED to BLUE ...
- ... whereas others are mixtures of dyes such as UNIVERSAL INDICATOR which ..
- ... show a RANGE OF COLOUR to indicate just how ACIDIC or ALKALINE a substance is.

THE pH SCALE

This measures the ACIDITY, ALKALINITY, or NEUTRALITY of a solution ...

... ACROSS A 14 POINT SCALE

VERY ACIDIC ↔					SLIGHTLY ACIDIC	NEUTRAL	SLIGHTLY ALKALINE ↔						VERY ALKALINE
1	2	3	4	5	6	7	8	9	10	11	12	13	14

When used with UNIVERSAL INDICATOR, we get the following range of colours:-

e.g. Battery Acid, Stomach Acid — Lemon Juice, Vinegar — Soda Water — Water — Soap — Baking Powder — Washing Soda — Oven Cleaner — Potassium Hydroxide

NEUTRALISATION

Basically, this occurs when the right amounts of acid and alkali react ...
... to "cancel" each other out to form a salt and water (which is NEUTRAL).

ACID + ALKALI ⟶ SALT + WATER

e.g. HCl	+	KOH	⟶	KCl	+	H_2O
HYDROCHLORIC ACID		POTASSIUM HYDROXIDE		POTASSIUM CHLORIDE		WATER
STRONG ACID, pH 1		STRONG ALKALI, pH 14				NEUTRAL, pH 7

EVERYDAY APPLICATIONS OF NEUTRALISATION

1. TREATMENT OF INDIGESTION: Too much acid production in the stomach can feel uncomfortable. Indigestion powders contain SODIUM HYDROGEN CARBONATE, and/or MAGNESIUM OXIDE to help to neutralise the excess acid.

2. TREATMENT OF ACIDIC SOILS: Excess acidity can cause crop failure, and alkalis can be "washed out" of soils by acid rain. CALCIUM HYDROXIDE ($Ca(OH)_2$) is added to neutralise the excess acidity.

3. TREATMENT OF WASP AND BEE STINGS: Wasp stings are alkaline and are treated by rubbing vinegar onto the sting. Bee stings are acidic and so sodium carbonate (indigestion powder) should be rubbed onto the skin.

1. What are indicators? Copy out the colours produced by universal indicator.
2. What is neutralisation? Write out the word equation for the neutralisation reaction between HCl and KOH.
3. Give three everyday applications of neutralisation reactions.

REACTION OF ACIDS WITH METALS

Metals which are above hydrogen in the reactivity series (see page 46) react with acids to produce HYDROGEN.

ACID + METAL → SALT + HYDROGEN

e.g. HYDROCHLORIC ACID + MAGNESIUM → MAGNESIUM CHLORIDE + HYDROGEN

* HYDRO<u>CHLORIC</u> ACID ALWAYS PRODUCES <u>CHLORIDE</u> SALTS.
* <u>SULPH</u>URIC ACID ALWAYS PRODUCES <u>SULPHATE</u> SALTS.

REACTION OF ACIDS WITH BASES

- Bases are the OXIDES and HYDROXIDES of METALS. Those which are SOLUBLE are called ALKALIS.
- INSOLUBLE and SOLUBLE BASES react with acids in the SAME WAY ...

ACID + BASE → SALT + WATER

e.g. SULPHURIC ACID + ZINC OXIDE (insoluble base) → ZINC SULPHATE + WATER

* HYDRO<u>CHLORIC</u> ACID ALWAYS PRODUCES <u>CHLORIDE</u> SALTS.
* <u>SULPH</u>URIC ACID ALWAYS PRODUCES <u>SULPHATE</u> SALTS.
* <u>NITR</u>IC ACID ALWAYS PRODUCES <u>NITRATE</u> SALTS.

REACTION OF ACIDS WITH CARBONATES

Carbonates will also neutralise acids ...

ACID + CARBONATE → SALT + WATER + CARBON DIOXIDE

e.g. HYDROCHLORIC ACID + CALCIUM CARBONATE → CALCIUM CHLORIDE + WATER + CARBON DIOXIDE

* HYDRO<u>CHLORIC</u> ACID ALWAYS PRODUCES <u>CHLORIDE</u> SALTS.
* <u>SULPH</u>URIC ACID ALWAYS PRODUCES <u>SULPHATE</u> SALTS.

WEATHERING AND CORROSION BY ACIDS

CARBON DIOXIDE, SULPHUR DIOXIDE and NITROGEN DIOXIDE formed as a result of burning both by industry and in car engines are able to dissolve in rain water to produce ACID RAIN. This is a fairly weak acid but has the following effects ...

1. Dissolves away buildings and statues which contain limestone.
2. Corrodes exposed metal work.
3. Carves out cave systems in limestone areas.
4. Weathers limestone rock generally. (And other types of rock to a lesser extent.)

1. Write out a suitable word equation for the reaction between a) an acid and a metal, b) an acid and a base and c) an acid and a carbonate (use different examples to those above).
2. Give four examples of how acid rain is causing weathering and corrosion to outdoor structures.

NAMING COMPOUNDS

Many people find this a confusing subject because there seems to be so many names. However the names are there to help if you follow some simple rules ...

"THE -IDE AND -ATE RULE"

If a COMPOUND ends in -IDE, then it means that it consists of just two elements joined together e.g. ...

Potassium chloride is two elements joined together, potassium and chlorine, KCl.
Magnesium sulphide is two elements joined together, magnesium and sulphur, MgS.
Calcium bromide is two elements joined together, calcium and bromine, $CaBr_2$.

If a COMPOUND ends in -ATE, then it means that it consists of two elements joined together, ... PLUS OXYGEN. e.g. ...

Sodium carbonate is two elements, sodium and carbon PLUS OXYGEN, joined together, Na_2CO_3.
Calcium sulphate is two elements, calcium and sulphur PLUS OXYGEN, joined together, $CaSO_4$.
Magnesium nitrate is two elements, magnesium and nitrogen PLUS OXYGEN, joined together, $Mg(NO_3)_2$.

HAZARD SYMBOLS

To be safe you should be able to recognise, and explain the significance of the following symbols:

Oxidising
These substances provide oxygen which allows other materials to burn more fiercely.

Highly flammable
These substances easily catch fire.

Toxic
These substances can cause death. They may have their effects when swallowed or breathed in or absorbed through the skin.

Harmful
These substances are similar to toxic substances but less dangerous.

Corrosive
These substances attack and destroy living tissues, including eyes and skin.

Irritant
These substances are not corrosive but can cause reddening or blistering of the skin.

THREE COMMON TESTS

You also need to know the common test for the following gases ...

No.1 OXYGEN

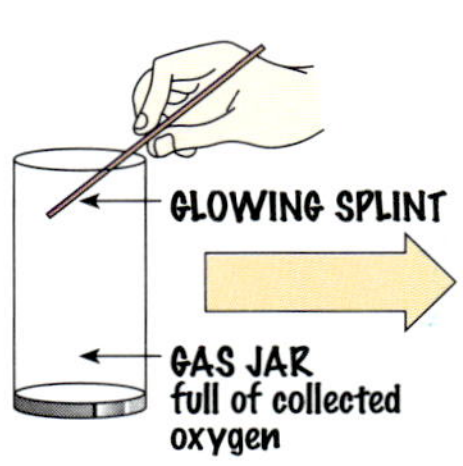

No.2 CARBON DIOXIDE

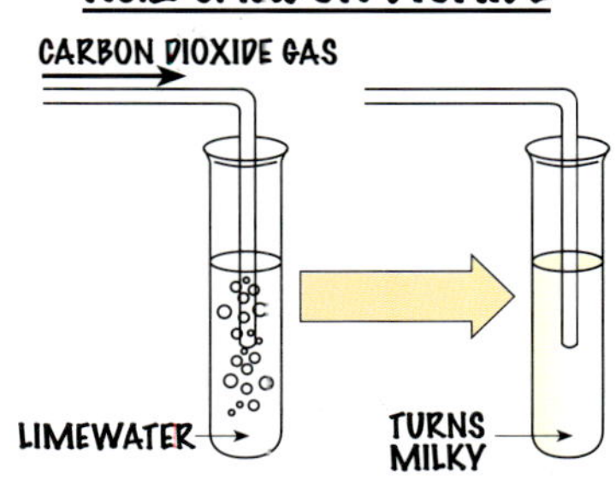

No.3 HYDROGEN

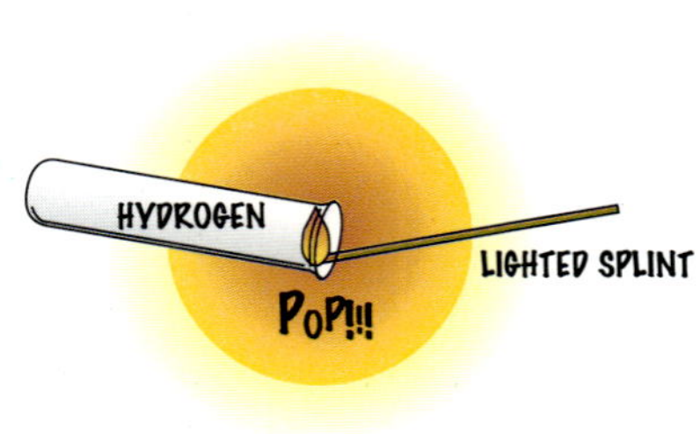

1. Give the names of the following compounds: KNO_3, CaF_2, and $MgCO_3$.
2. Write the formulae of Sodium chloride and Potassium sulphate.

1 A material which is used for a particular job needs to have properties which make it suitable.

Property	Description	Example
FLEXIBILITY	CAN BE STRETCHED BUT WILL GO BACK TO ORIGINAL SHAPE	REINFORCED CONCRETE
HARDNESS	CAN BE BENT EASILY WITHOUT BREAKING	RUBBER
STRENGTH	CANNOT HAVE IT'S SHAPE CHANGED VERY EASILY	SPRING
ELASTICITY	DIFFICULT TO BREAK WHEN STRETCHED OR SQUEEZED	DIAMOND

Complete the above diagram, linking the description and the example to the property. One has been done for you.

2 a) Describe a simple experiment to show whether a material is an electrical conductor or insulator.

b) Here are EIGHT materials.

WOOD	ALUMINIUM	COPPER	GLASS	POLYTHENE
	PERSPEX	GOLD	RUSTY METAL	

Which of the above are electrical conductors?

3 In the space below draw a diagram to show the arrangement of particles in:

SOLID LIQUID GAS

4 a) What is diffusion?

b) Below are TWO gas jars, one containing Oxygen gas and the other Bromine gas (diagram A). Complete diagram B and diagram C which show the two gas jars at two later times.

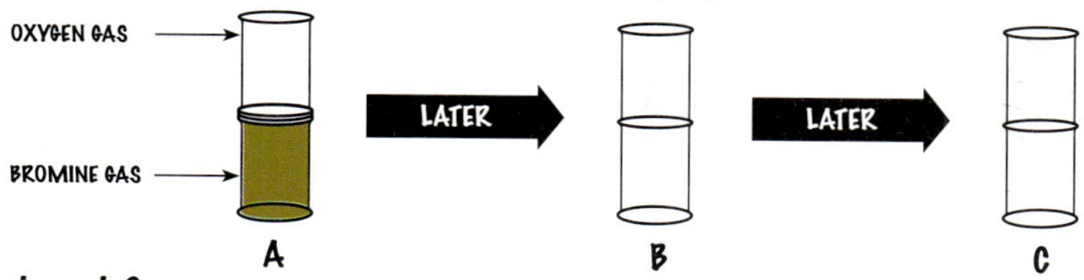

5 a) What is the rock cycle?

b) What is the name of the process whereby rocks at the surface of the Earth get broken up?

c) Name the THREE types of rock?

d) Which rock is formed from liquid rock called Magma?

e) Which rock is formed from layers of sediment?

f) Which rocks are formed from compression and heating of rocks which are formed from layers of sediment?

6 Below are TWO simple experiments which show oil being added to paraffin and water.

a) Complete the diagrams.

b) What does this experiment show?

c) Explain why a car mechanic would be very interested in the results of the experiments above.

7 a) What is a PHYSICAL CHANGE? Give one example.

b) What is a CHEMICAL CHANGE? Give one example.

c) Which of the following are physical changes:

MAKING BRICKS FROM CLAY	MELTING ICE	DISSOLVING SALT IN WATER	BURNING A CANDLE

8 a) What is a thermal decomposition reaction?

Below is a simple experiment to show the thermal decomposition of silver oxide.

b) Write a word equation for the chemical reaction that has taken place.

c) The oxygen given off in the reaction can be collected.

How can we test that this gas is oxygen?

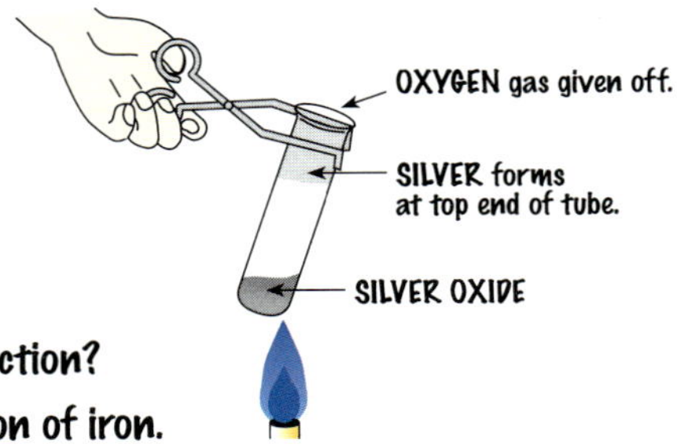

9 a) What is reduction?

b) Why is the production of Iron a reduction reaction?

c) Write out the word equation for the production of iron.

d) What is the name of the reduction process that produces aluminium from it's oxide?

10 Below are TWO lit bunsen burners.

Bunsen Burner A

Bunsen Burner B

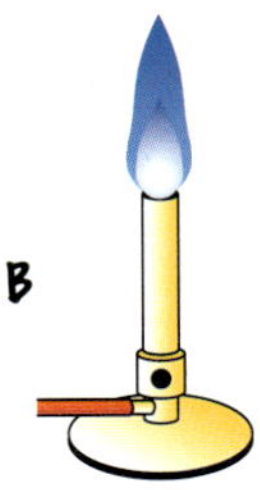

a) Why are the two flames different in colour?

b) Which flame is the hottest?

c) The fuel burned in the bunsen burner is methane. Write out the word equation for the burning of methane.

d) One of the waste products of the burning of any fuel (including methane) is partly responsible for Global Warming. What is the name of the waste product and what is Global Warming?

11 a) In the diagram, an iron nail is placed in copper sulphate solution. Explain what you would expect to happen (iron is higher in the reactivity series than copper).

b) If a silver necklace was placed in the copper sulphate solution. Explain what you would expect to happen (silver is lower than copper in the reactivity series).

c) Gold is very near the bottom of the reactivity series. Explain why gold is mined as a pure element rather than as an ore.

12 a) An unknown substance turns red litmus blue, and blue litmus stays blue on contact.

Is the substance ACID, ALKALINE or NEUTRAL?

b) An unknown substance has no effect on red litmus. What can you say about this substance?

c) A bee sting is acidic. Which of these would you rub into the skin after being stung?

SODIUM CARBONATE | VINEGAR | WATER

13 a) Complete this equation:

ACID + ALKALI ⟶ ______ + ______

b) Look at this equation:

HYDROCHLORIC ACID + MAGNESIUM ⟶ MAGNESIUM CHLORIDE + HYDROGEN

The salt formed here is a CHLORIDE. What change would you have to make if you wanted to produce a SULPHATE?

c) Complete this equation:

ACID + CARBONATE ⟶ ______ + ______ + ______

14 a) Magnesium reacts with sulphur to form magnesium sulphide. What is the formula of magnesium sulphide?

b) Which substance is represented by the formula $CaCO_3$?

c) Which gas would be given off if this substance was heated strongly?

STATIC ELECTRICITY

- TWO MATERIALS can become CHARGED by FRICTION when ...
- ... they are RUBBED AGAINST EACH OTHER.
- The materials must be INSULATORS and we say ...
- ... that the materials have become charged with **STATIC ELECTRICITY,** meaning ...
- ... that the electricity stays on the material and doesn't move.

HERE ARE TWO WAYS YOU CAN 'GENERATE' STATIC ELECTRICITY.

COMBING YOUR HAIR

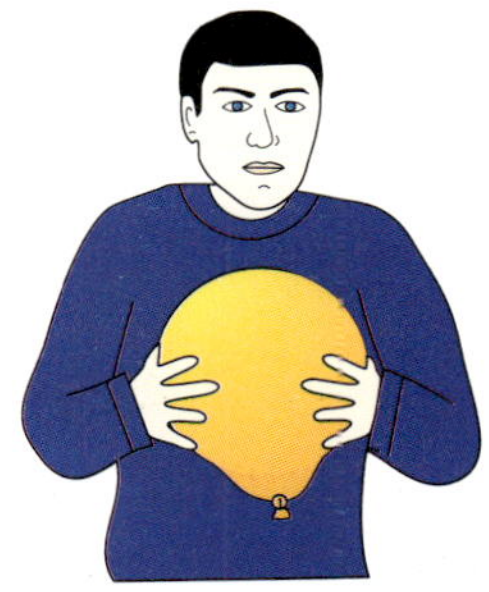

RUBBING A BALLOON AGAINST A JUMPER

WHY MATERIALS BECOME CHARGED

If TWO materials are rubbed together and become CHARGED then ...

- ... ELECTRONS are 'scraped off' one material and ...
- ... put on the other material leaving ...
- ... ONE of the MATERIALS **NEGATIVELY CHARGED** and ...
- ... the OTHER MATERIAL **POSITIVELY CHARGED.**

POLYTHENE ROD RUBBED WITH A CLOTH

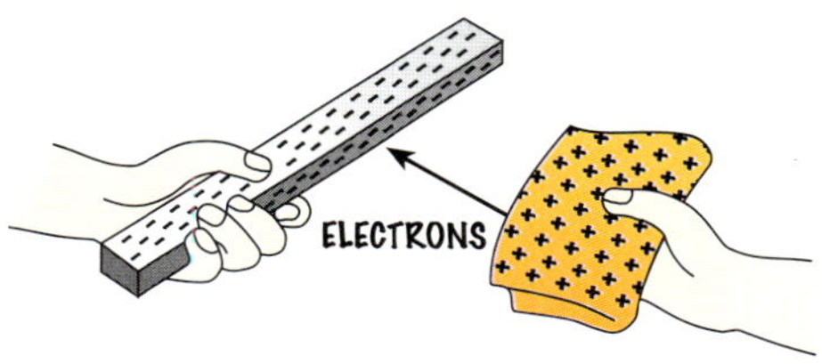

Polythene GAINS electrons ...
... NEGATIVELY CHARGED.

Cloth LOSES electrons ...
... POSITIVELY CHARGED.

PERSPEX ROD RUBBED WITH A CLOTH

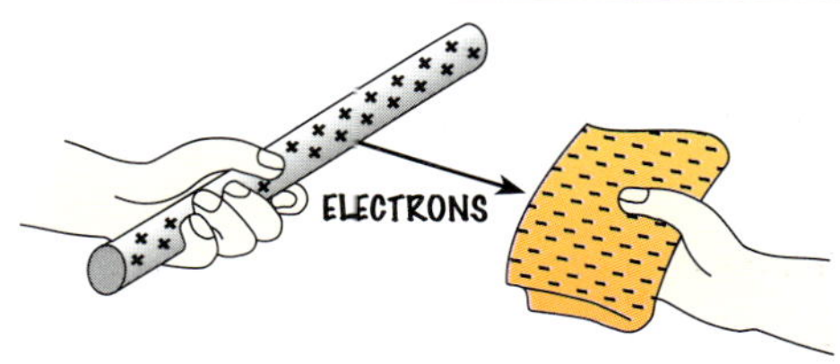

Perspex LOSES electrons ...
... POSITIVELY CHARGED.

Cloth GAINS electrons ...
... NEGATIVELY CHARGED.

REPULSION AND ATTRACTION BETWEEN CHARGED MATERIALS

Very simply ... TWO MATERIALS WITH THE SAME CHARGE ON THEM, REPEL EACH OTHER while ...
... TWO MATERIALS WITH DIFFERENT CHARGE ON THEM, ATTRACT EACH OTHER.

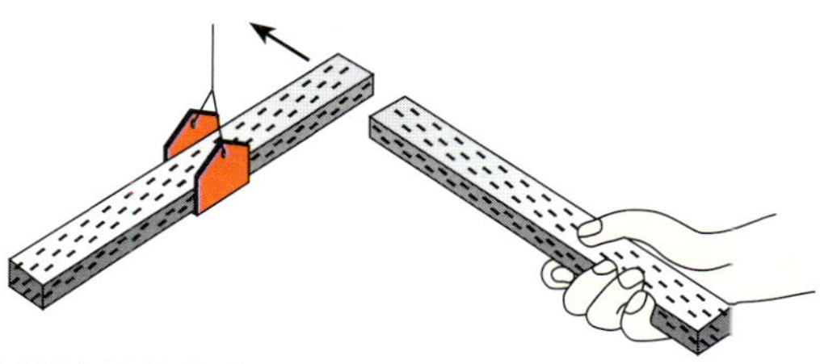

- The SUSPENDED POLYTHENE ROD ...
- ... is REPELLED by the HELD POLYTHENE ROD.

NB. WE WOULD GET THE SAME WITH PERSPEX RODS.

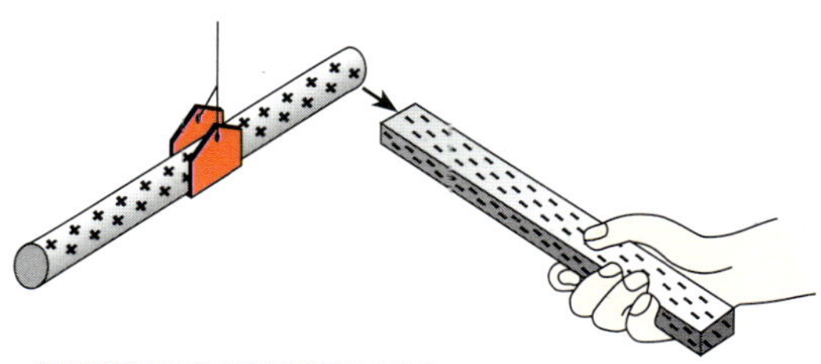

- The SUSPENDED PERSPEX ROD ...
- ... is ATTRACTED by the HELD POLYTHENE ROD.

NB. WE WOULD GET THE SAME IF THE RODS WERE THE OTHER WAY AROUND.

1. Describe STATIC ELECTRICITY and explain why the charged materials must be insulators? 2. Explain (using diagrams) why a polythene rod becomes negatively charged and a cloth becomes positively charged when they are rubbed together.
3. What is the simple rule as to whether TWO charged materials will REPEL or ATTRACT each other. Draw a diagram to show what happens with TWO positively charged perspex rods.

SIMPLE CIRCUITS

ALL electrical circuits have ...

- ... a CELL, BATTERY or POWER SUPPLY to provide the ELECTRICAL ENERGY and ...
- ... ELECTRICAL DEVICES (COMPONENTS) which need this energy to make them work.

WHAT IT IS	CELL or BATTERY	BULB	SWITCH
WHAT IT LOOKS LIKE			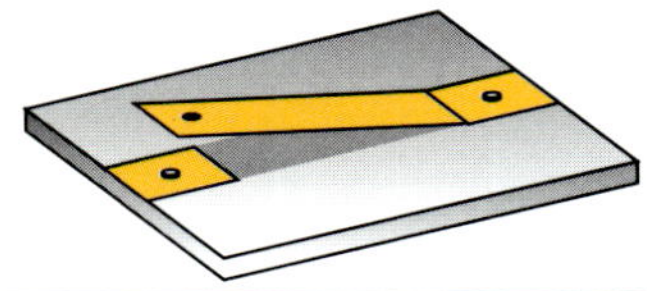
HOW WE DRAW IT'S SYMBOL	OR IF THERE IS MORE THAN ONE	OR	OPEN CLOSED
WHAT IT DOES	SUPPLIES THE ELECTRICAL ENERGY	CHANGES ELEC. ENERGY INTO LIGHT ENERGY	SWITCHES THE CIRCUIT 'ON' OR 'OFF'

DRAWING CIRCUITS FROM DIAGRAMS

These often look complicated but follow this simple rule ...

- DRAW YOUR BATTERY AND THEN WORK YOUR WAY AROUND FROM ONE END OF THE BATTERY ...
- ... TO THE OTHER END, DRAWING THE DEVICES AS YOU GO ALONG.

1

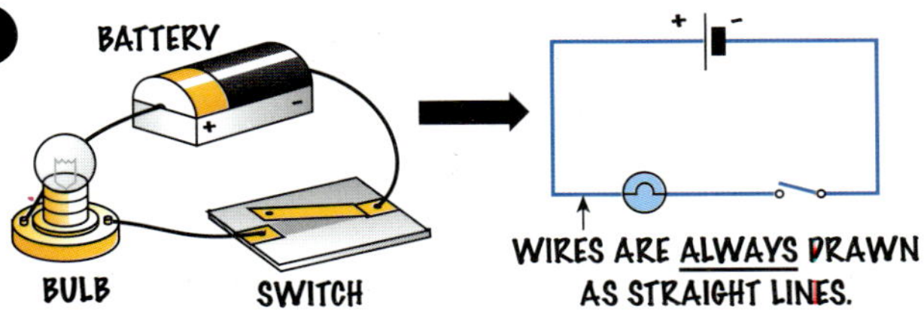

2

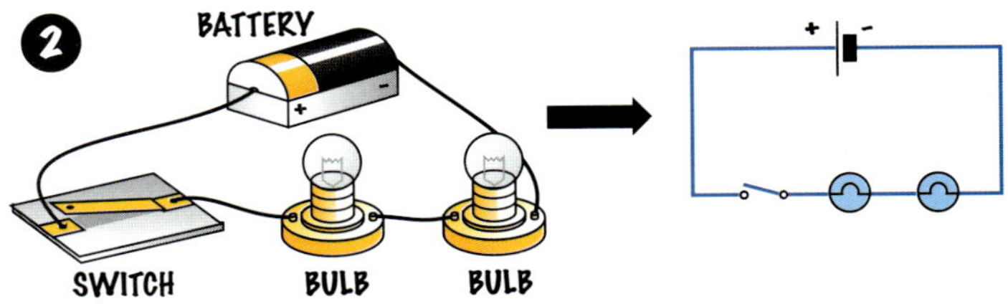

HOW SWITCHES CONTROL ELECTRICAL DEVICES

Below are SIX circuits, each containing a CELL, TWO BULBS (A and B) and TWO SWITCHES.
For a BULB to be 'ON' it must be PART OF A COMPLETE CIRCUIT otherwise the BULB is 'OFF'.

1

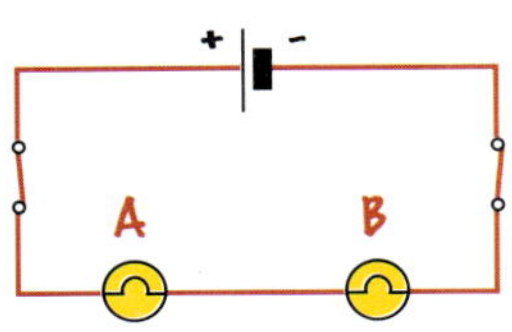

COMPLETE CIRCUIT.
BOTH BULBS ON.

2

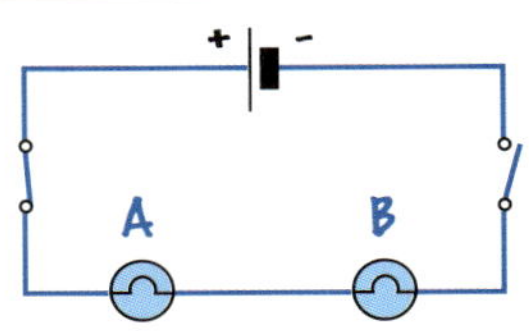

INCOMPLETE CIRCUIT.
BOTH BULBS OFF.

3

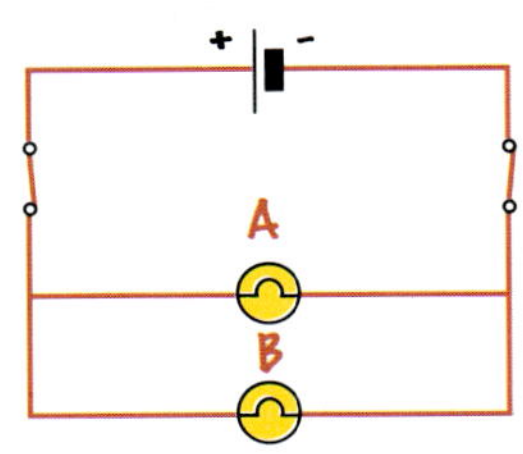

BOTH CIRCUITS COMPLETE.
BOTH BULBS ON.

4

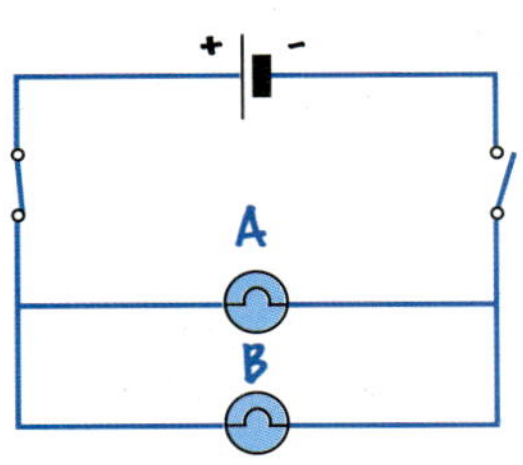

BOTH CIRCUITS INCOMPLETE.
BOTH BULBS OFF.

5

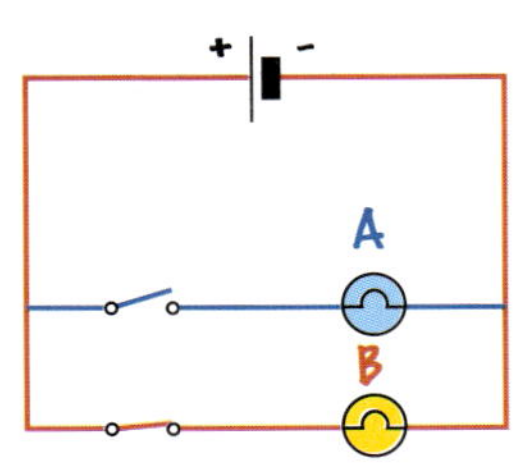

CIRCUIT A INCOMPLETE. BULB A OFF.
CIRCUIT B COMPLETE. BULB B ON.

6

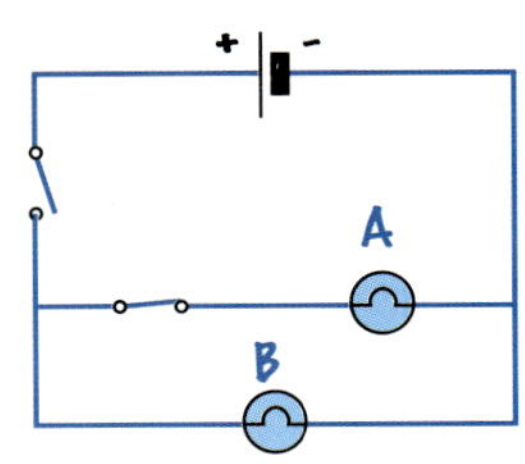

BOTH CIRCUITS INCOMPLETE.
BOTH BULBS OFF.

NB. There are OTHER electrical devices you may see in a circuit instead of the bulb ...
... e.g. MOTOR -Ⓜ-, BUZZER, but they will only work when they are PART OF A COMPLETE CIRCUIT.

1. Draw the symbols for a CELL, BATTERY of 3 CELLS, BULB and a SWITCH and explain what each one does.
2. Draw the SIX circuits just above using a pencil and ruler. Draw in RED any complete circuits and in BLUE any incomplete circuits.

ELECTRIC CURRENT

As we have seen a battery is a provider of electrical energy to the components in a circuit. This energy is carried around the circuit by ELECTRONS and the more 'powerful' the battery is, the more energy these electrons carry.

- This FLOW of ELECTRONS around the circuit is called an **ELECTRIC CURRENT** and ...
- ... it can be measured by using an **AMMETER.**
- Electric current is measured in AMPS (A).

Ammeter

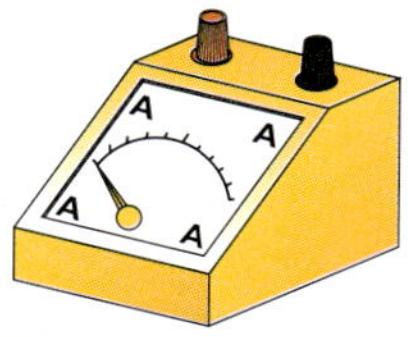

Symbol

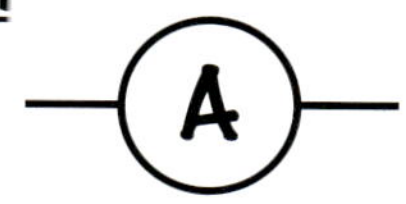

Remember
- The BIGGER THE READING ...
- ... the BIGGER THE CURRENT ...
- ... the MORE ENERGY THAT IS PROVIDED.

MEASURING CURRENT IN SERIES AND PARALLEL CIRCUITS

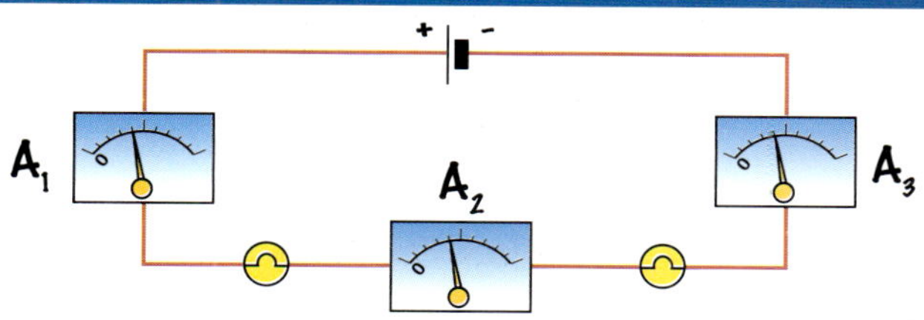

In a **SERIES CIRCUIT** the CURRENT readings ...
- ... A_1, A_2 and A_3 are ALL THE SAME proving ...
- ... that current does not get 'used up' ...
- ... by components (the bulbs) in the circuit ...
- ... but flows through each one in turn.

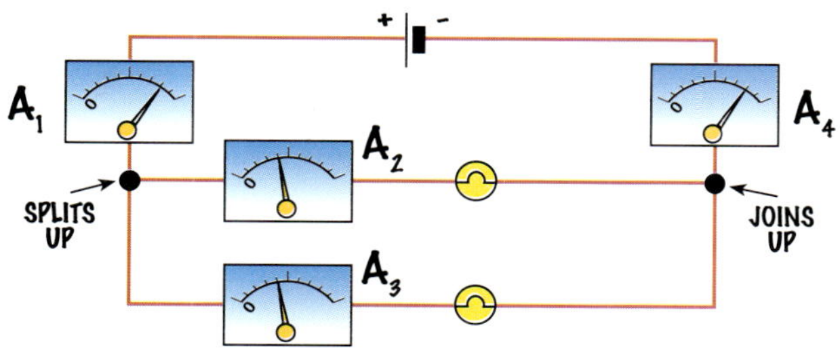

In a **PARALLEL CIRCUIT** the CURRENT A_1 ...
- ... splits up into A_2 and A_3 which ...
- ... then join up to give A_4 where ...
- ... $A_1 = A_2 + A_3 = A_4$.
- Again this proves that current does not get 'used up'.

CURRENT IN SERIES CIRCUITS

The amount of current in a series circuit depends on ...
1. SIZE OF BATTERY (NUMBER OF CELLS).
2. NUMBER AND TYPE OF COMPONENTS IN THE CIRCUIT.

- BULB AT NORMAL BRIGHTNESS.
- ONE CELL TO ONE BULB.

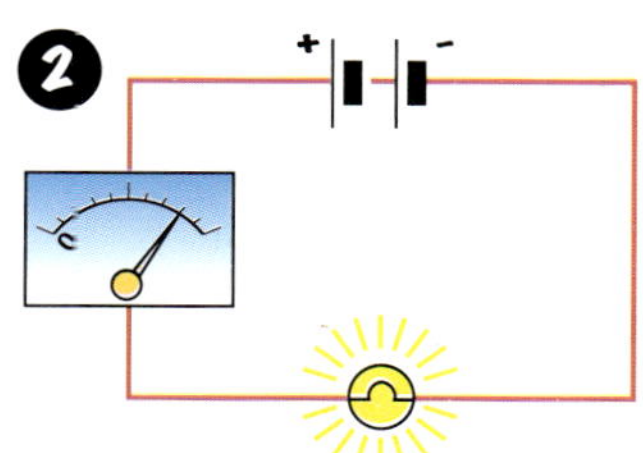

- BULB BRIGHTER as ...
- ... TWO CELLS TO ONE BULB.
- CURRENT TWICE THAT OF No.1.

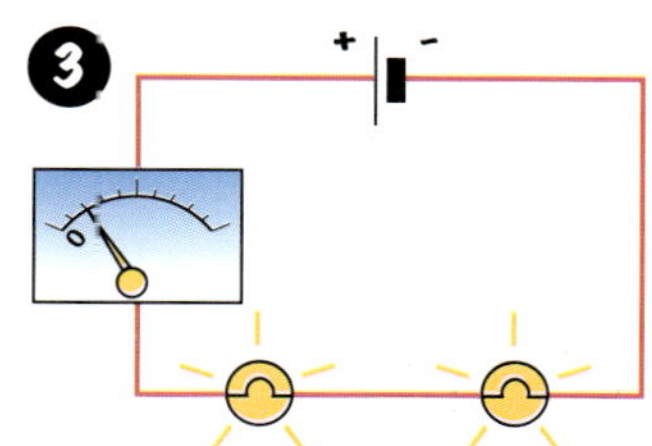

- BULBS DIMMER as ...
- ... ONE CELL TO TWO BULBS.
- CURRENT HALF THAT OF No. 1.

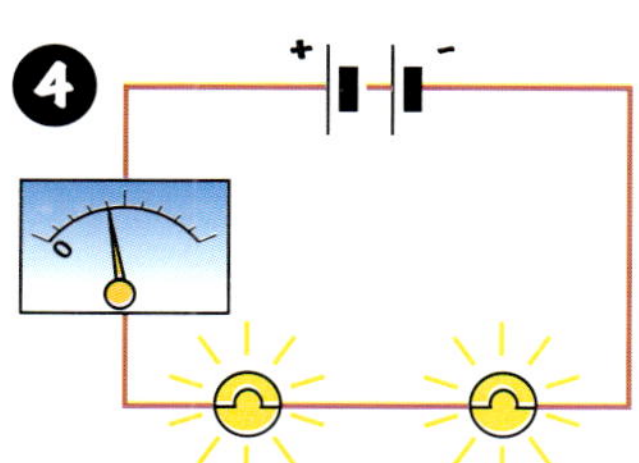

- BULBS AT NORMAL BRIGHTNESS as ...
- ... ONE CELL TO ONE BULB.
- CURRENT SAME AS No.1.

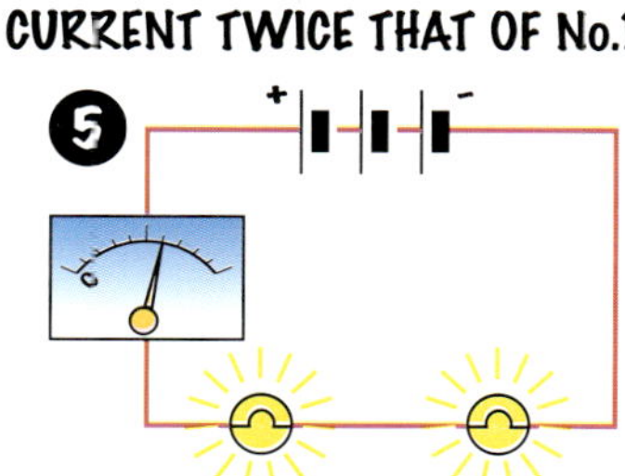

- BULBS BRIGHTER THAN No.1 as ...
- ... ONE AND A HALF CELLS TO ONE BULB.
- CURRENT 1½ x THAT OF No.1.

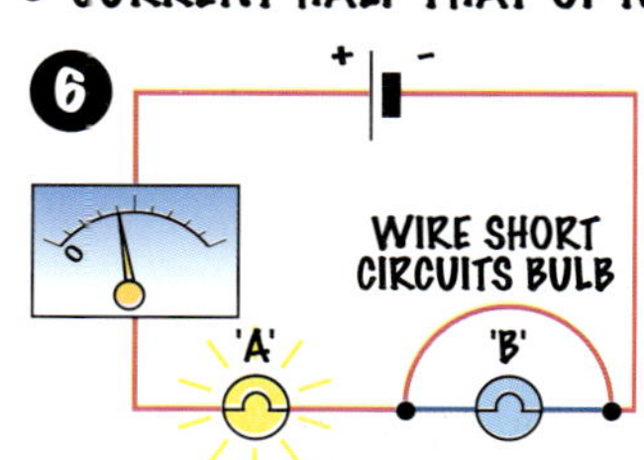

- BULB 'B' IS OFF (SHORT CIRCUITED) so ...
- ... ONE CELL TO ONE BULB.
- CURRENT SAME AS No.1.

1. What is an ELECTRIC CURRENT and how is it measured?
2. Draw a SERIES and PARALLEL circuit as above including the ammeters. If the reading on A_1 in both circuits is 6 Amps, draw in readings on the other ammeters. Explain your readings. 3. Draw the simple circuit as in No.1 just above. Draw THREE more circuits where the ammeter reading is i) ¼ x ii) ½ x iii) 2 x that at No.1.

MAGNETIC FIELDS

ALL MAGNETS have a **REGION OF SPACE AROUND THEM** ...
- ... called the **MAGNETIC FIELD** ...
- ... which exerts a **FORCE** ...
- ... on any **MAGNETIC MATERIAL** which enters it.

MAGNETIC FIELD AROUND A BAR MAGNET

A **BAR MAGNET** has a **PERMANENT MAGNETIC FIELD** around it ...
- ... which means, that the magnetic field is always there.

> The **ENDS** of a **BAR MAGNET** ...
> ... are called **POLES**.
> One end is the **NORTH (N) POLE** ...
> ... and the other is the **SOUTH (S) POLE**.

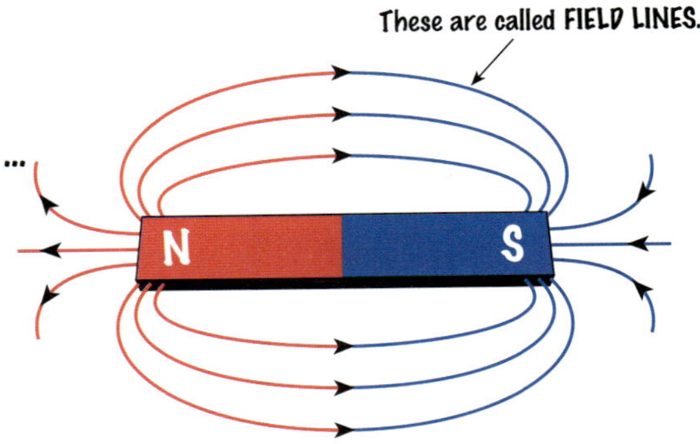

FORCES OF REPULSION AND ATTRACTION BETWEEN MAGNETS

When the **ENDS** of **TWO MAGNETS** are brought near to each other so that **THEIR MAGNETIC FIELDS OVERLAP** ...
- ... the two magnets will **REPEL EACH OTHER** if the **ENDS** have the **SAME POLES** while ...

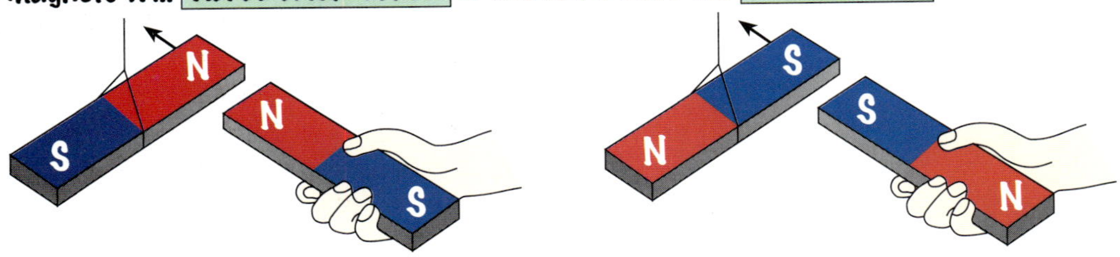

- ... if the **ENDS** have **DIFFERENT POLES** the two magnets will **ATTRACT EACH OTHER**.

This can be used to determine the poles of a magnet if they are unknown by simply ...
- ... bringing **ONE END** of the **UNKNOWN MAGNET** next to the **NORTH POLE** of a **KNOWN MAGNET**.
- If **REPULSION** occurs, that end is a **NORTH POLE** and the other end is a **SOUTH POLE** while ...
- ... if **ATTRACTION** occurs that end is a **SOUTH POLE** and the other end is a **NORTH POLE**.

FORCES OF ATTRACTION BETWEEN MAGNETS AND MAGNETIC MATERIALS

Eventually ...
- ... the **IRON BAR** is **ATTRACTED TOWARDS THE MAGNET**.
- The **END NEARER THE MAGNET** becomes a **SOUTH POLE** and the **OTHER END** a **NORTH POLE** (behaves like a magnet) while ...
- ... the **IRON PINS** are **ATTRACTED TOWARDS THE 'MAGNETISED' IRON BAR** and again ...
- ... the **ENDS NEARER THE IRON BAR** become **SOUTH POLES** and the **OTHER ENDS NORTH POLES**.

1. What is a **MAGNETIC FIELD**?
2. Draw the magnetic field around a bar magnet. Why is it a permanent magnetic field?
3. What is the simple rule as to whether the **ENDS** of **TWO** magnets will **REPEL** or **ATTRACT** each other.
4. How is it possible to determine the **POLES** of an unknown magnet? Draw diagrams to explain your answer.

THE FIELD PRODUCED BY AN ELECTROMAGNET

- If an ELECTRIC CURRENT flows through a COIL OF WIRE ...
- ... a MAGNETIC FIELD is FORMED AROUND THE COIL ...
- ... creating an ELECTROMAGNET which is ...
- ... a MAGNET that can be SWITCHED ON AND OFF.

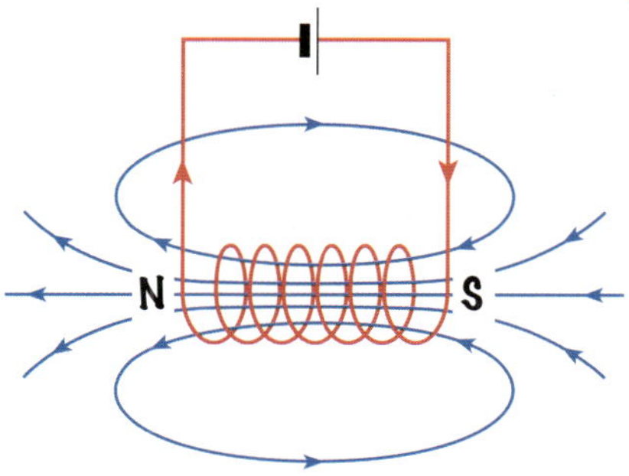

- The MAGNETIC FIELD formed is ...
- ... very SIMILAR to a BAR MAGNET ...

  ... and so ...
- ... ONE END OF THE COIL BECOMES A NORTH POLE and ...
- ... the OTHER END BECOMES A SOUTH POLE.

INCREASING THE NUMBER OF COILS, INCREASING THE ELECTRIC CURRENT AND PLACING A PIECE OF IRON INSIDE THE COIL INCREASES THE STRENGTH OF THE ELECTROMAGNET.

HOW WE USE ELECTROMAGNETS I

Electromagnets are found in many devices. • Here are TWO:

1. THE ELECTRIC BELL

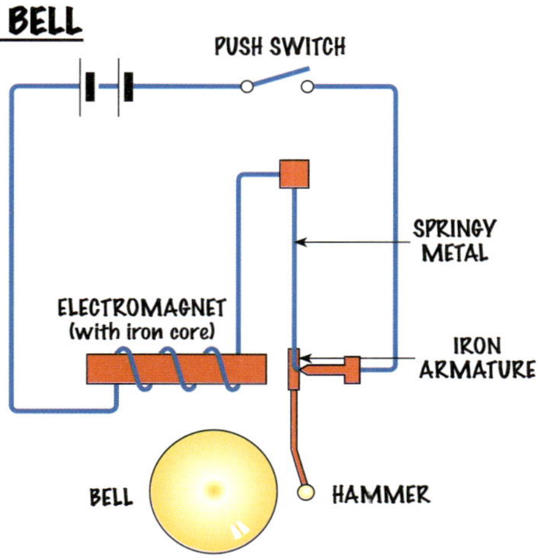

- When the PUSH SWITCH is CLOSED ...
- ... the CIRCUIT is COMPLETED and ...
- ... a CURRENT flows ...
- ... switching ON the ELECTROMAGNET.
- The IRON ARMATURE is PULLED TOWARDS IT and ...
- ... the HAMMER hits the BELL.

However ...
- ... as soon as the IRON ARMATURE is PULLED ...
- ... the CIRCUIT is BROKEN and ...
- ... NO CURRENT flows ...
- ... SWITCHING OFF the ELECTROMAGNET.

Resulting in ...
- ... the IRON ARMATURE GOING BACK ...
- ... COMPLETING the CIRCUIT and ...
- ... everything starts again ...

HOW WE USE ELECTROMAGNETS II

2. THE RELAY

A RELAY is a SWITCH where a SMALL CURRENT SWITCHES ON A LARGER CURRENT (FOR SAFETY).

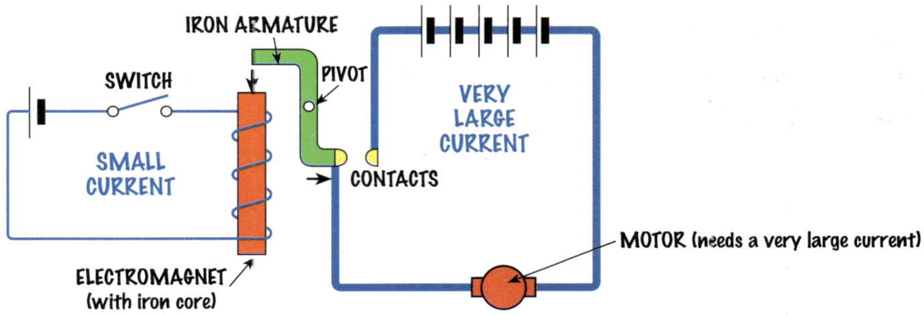

- When the SWITCH is CLOSED, a SMALL CURRENT flows and the ELECTROMAGNET is SWITCHED ON.
- The PIVOTED IRON ARMATURE is PULLED TOWARDS the ELECTROMAGNET ...
- ... causing the CONTACTS TO CLOSE.
- The second circuit is now complete and a LARGE CURRENT CAN NOW FLOW.

1. What is an ELECTROMAGNET?
2. Draw the magnetic field formed around a coil of wire when an electric current passes through the coil. What happens to this magnetic field when the current is switched off?
3. Draw fully labelled diagrams with complete explanations of TWO ways in which electromagnets are used in devices.

A FORCE is a ... **PUSH**

... or a **PULL**

- They are measured in NEWTONS (N) ...
- ... and act in a particular direction.

THREE IMPORTANT FORCES IN ACTION

1. WEIGHT

- This is the force that acts on ALL OBJECTS because ...
- ... of the gravitational attraction between them and the earth.

A GIRL

A CAR

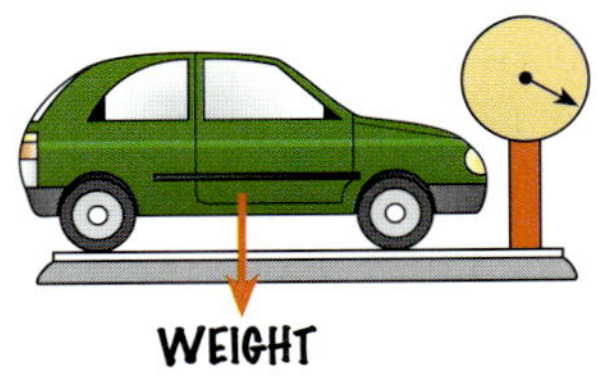

2. FRICTION

- This is the force that PUSHES against a MOVING OBJECT ...
- ... and tries to SLOW IT DOWN.
- Friction is created whenever TWO TOUCHING OBJECTS or SURFACES MOVE PAST EACH OTHER.

A MOVING CYCLIST

(NB. Force of WEIGHT also acts on the cyclist, but we've not included it on the diagram).

3. AIR RESISTANCE

- This is the force that PUSHES against a MOVING OBJECT AS IT PASSES THROUGH AIR.
- As for friction, AIR RESISTANCE tries to SLOW DOWN the moving object.
- The greater the air resistance, the greater the slowing down.

A PARACHUTIST

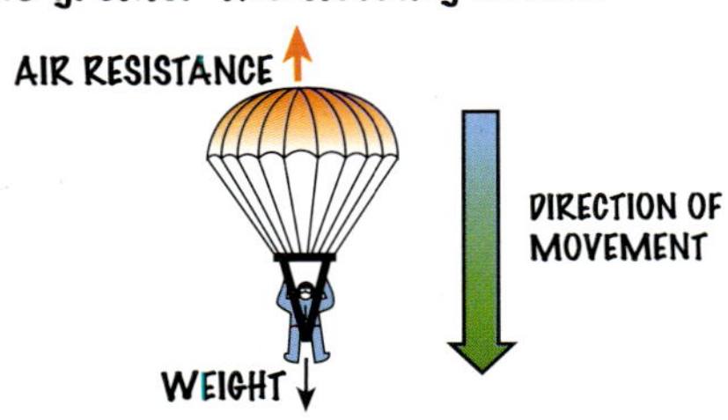

(NB. We've included the force of WEIGHT on this diagram as it is a RELEVANT FORCE).

FORCES DUE TO STRETCHING AND SQUEEZING

STRETCHING

A STRETCHED SPRING or ELASTIC BAND EXERTS A FORCE on WHATEVER is STRETCHING THEM.

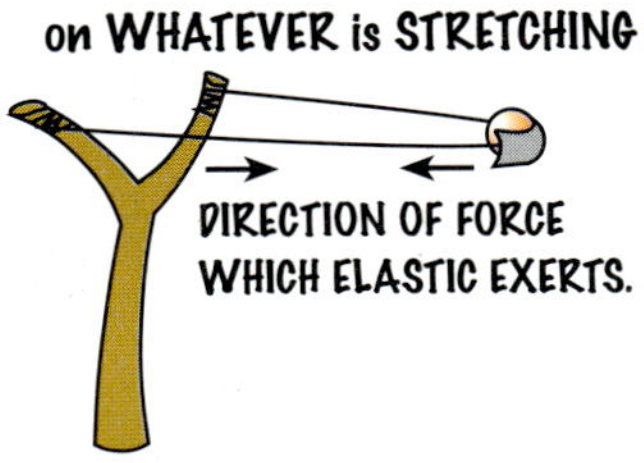

SQUEEZING

A SQUEEZED (COMPRESSED) SPRING EXERTS A FORCE ON WHATEVER IS SQUEEZING IT.

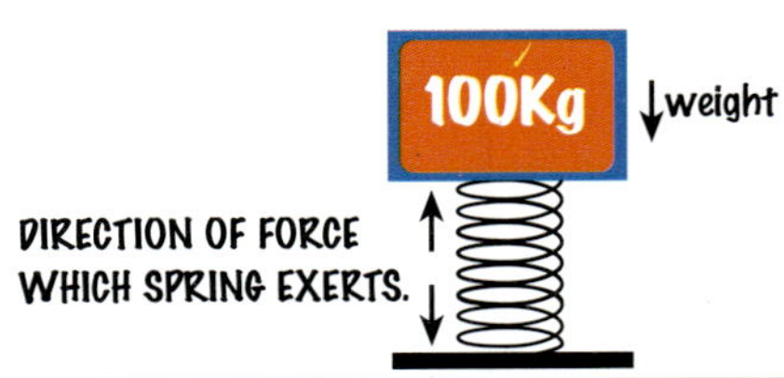

1. What is a force? What are they measured in? 2. Draw diagrams to show these 3 important forces in action: WEIGHT, FRICTION and AIR RESISTANCE. 3. Draw diagrams to show a) the force an elastic band exerts when it is stretched b) the force a spring exerts when it is compressed.

EFFECT ON MOVEMENT

You need to know the effect of BALANCED and UNBALANCED FORCES ...

... on STATIONARY (STILL) and MOVING OBJECTS.

		If the FORCES on the object are ...	
		... BALANCED ...	... UNBALANCED ...
... and the object is ...	... STATIONARY ...	... then the object will REMAIN STATIONARY.	... then the object will ACCELERATE/DECELERATE or CHANGE DIRECTION.
	... MOVING AT CONSTANT SPEED ...	... then the object will CONTINUE AT THE SAME CONSTANT SPEED.	... then the object will ACCELERATE/DECELERATE or CHANGE DIRECTION.

A TYPICAL EXAMPLE

The driver has unfortunately run out of petrol and needs some help ...
... from these kind children who just happened to be passing.

With just one child pushing, ...
THE PUSH FORCE IS EQUAL TO THE FRICTIONAL FORCE, ...
and so the FORCES ARE BALANCED and the STATIONARY CAR ...
... REMAINS STATIONARY.

With two children now pushing, ...
THE PUSH FORCE IS GREATER THAN THE FRICTIONAL FORCE, ...
and so the FORCES ARE UNBALANCED and the STATIONARY CAR ...
... will now START TO MOVE AND ACCELERATE.

When one child drops out, ...
THE PUSH FORCE IS EQUAL TO THE FRICTIONAL FORCE AGAIN,
but these BALANCED FORCES will keep the MOVING CAR ...
... moving AT THE SAME CONSTANT SPEED.

With the petrol pump getting nearer, the other child drops out, ...
making the PUSH FORCE LESS THAN THE FRICTIONAL FORCE,
and making the FORCES UNBALANCED. This causes ...
... the car to DECELERATE AND EVENTUALLY STOP.

EFFECT ON DIRECTION OF MOVEMENT

- Besides changing the speed of an object, ...
- ... UNBALANCED FORCES CAN ALSO CHANGE THE DIRECTION OF MOVEMENT.
- When the footballer kicks the ball as soon as it reaches him ...
- ... he causes UNBALANCED FORCES to act on the ball which ...
- ... cause a CHANGE OF DIRECTION, even though the speed of the ball may remain unchanged.

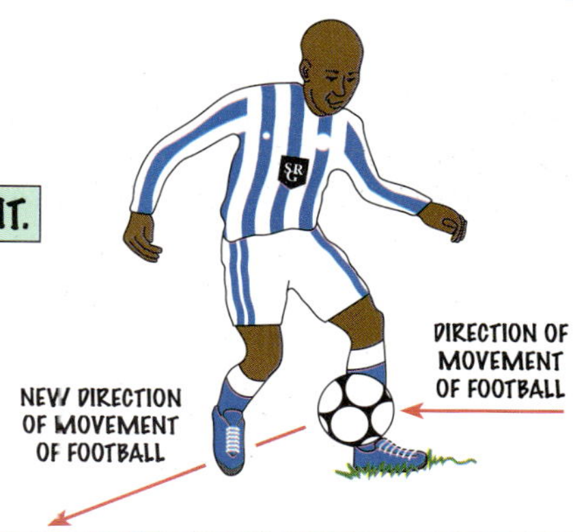

1. What effect do BALANCED FORCES have on a) a stationary object b) an object moving at constant speed?
2. What effect do UNBALANCED FORCES have on a) a stationary object b) an object moving at constant speed?
3. Give THREE examples of how UNBALANCED FORCES can change the DIRECTION OF MOVEMENT of an object.

PRESSURE, FORCE AND AREA

- PRESSURE is exerted whenever ...
- ... a FORCE is applied over an AREA.

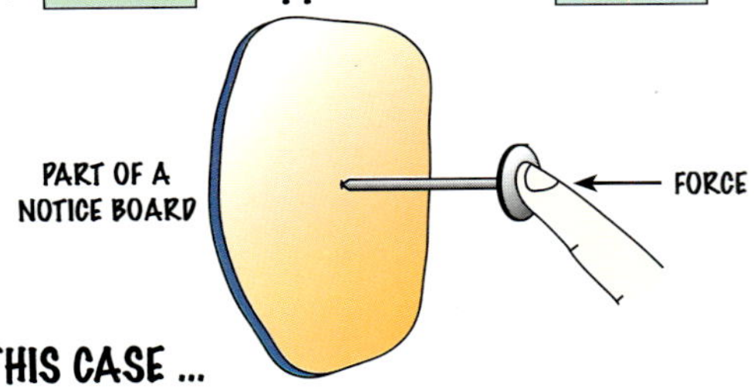

IN THIS CASE ...

- The finger applies FORCE onto the HEAD of the PIN.
- This force is then APPLIED by the POINT of the PIN ...
- ... onto a VERY SMALL AREA ...
- ... creating a VERY LARGE PRESSURE.
- The PIN is PUSHED into the notice board.

SAME FINGER ...
... SAME FORCE ...
... NO PIN!

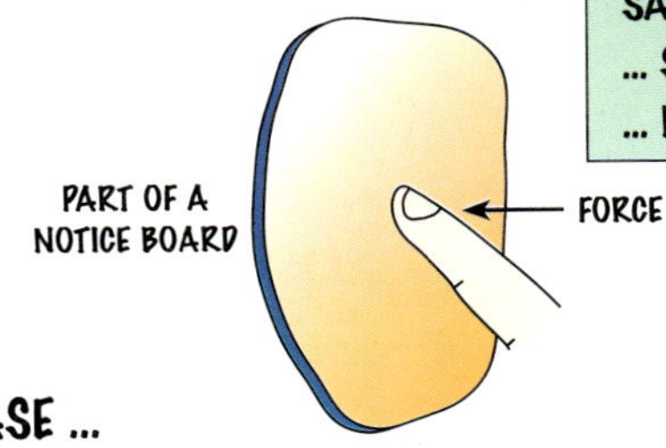

IN THIS CASE ...

- The finger now applies the same FORCE ...
- ... onto a VERY LARGE AREA (compared to the pin point) ...
- ... creating a VERY SMALL PRESSURE.
- FINGER CANNOT BE PUSHED into the notice board.

The relationship between pressure, force and area is:

$$\text{PRESSURE} = \frac{\text{FORCE}}{\text{AREA}}$$

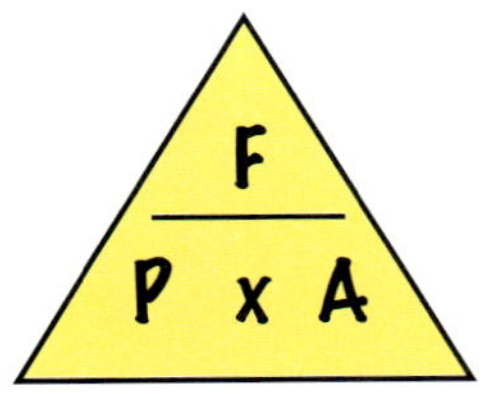

THIS IS A FORMULA TRIANGLE

Pressure is measured in ...

- Newtons per millimetre squared (N/mm^2)
- Newtons per centimetre squared (N/cm^2)
- Newtons per metre squared (N/m^2)

EXAMPLES

1. The above pin is pressed into the board with a force of 30N. The point of the pin has an area of $0.2mm^2$, what is the pressure exerted by the point onto the board?

Using our relationship: $\text{PRESSURE} = \frac{\text{FORCE}}{\text{AREA}} = \frac{30N}{0.2mm^2} = 150N/mm^2$

2. If the finger on its own was to exert the SAME pressure onto the board, what force would the finger have to apply if the end of the finger has an area of $200mm^2$?

Using our relationship: FORCE = PRESSURE x AREA
(which is rearranged using formula triangle)

$= 150N/mm^2 \times 200mm^2$
$= 30,000N$
(= A BROKEN FINGER!)

APPLICATIONS OF PRESSURE

The amount of PRESSURE EXERTED on a SURFACE has some important practical applications in various situations.

Examples

1. SHARP KNIFE BLADES
Makes it easier to 'CUT THROUGH' food.

2. ICE SKATERS
Cause ICE to MELT at AREA of CONTACT, easier to skate.

Examples

1. SNOW SHOES AND SKIS
To prevent SINKING INTO THE SNOW.

2. FOUNDATION OF BUILDINGS
To prevent building SINKING INTO THE GROUND.

1. What is PRESSURE? Write out the formula and the formula triangle.
2. A woman of weight 600N stands on ONE stiletto heel of area $2cm^2$. What pressure does she exert on the ground?
3. If a man is to exert the SAME PRESSURE when standing on ONE FOOT of area $150cm^2$. What is his weight?
4. Explain why a) snow shoes have a LARGE AREA and b) knife blades are made sharp to have a SMALL AREA.

MEASURING MOMENTS

- Forces can be used ...
- ... to TURN OBJECTS ABOUT A PIVOT.

Consider the situation where a boy is trying to unscrew a nut using a spanner.

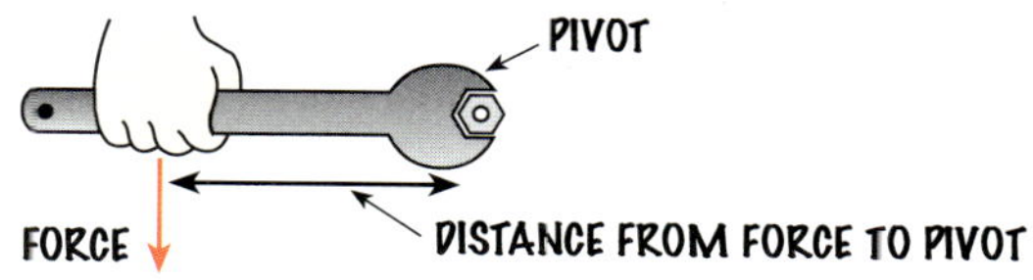

- The SPANNER exerts a MOMENT or a TURNING FORCE on the nut.
- If the MOMENT is BIG ENOUGH, it will unscrew the nut ...
- ... if it's not, there are TWO ways of INCREASING the MOMENT.

1. INCREASE DISTANCE FROM FORCE TO PIVOT ...

... use a spanner with a longer handle.

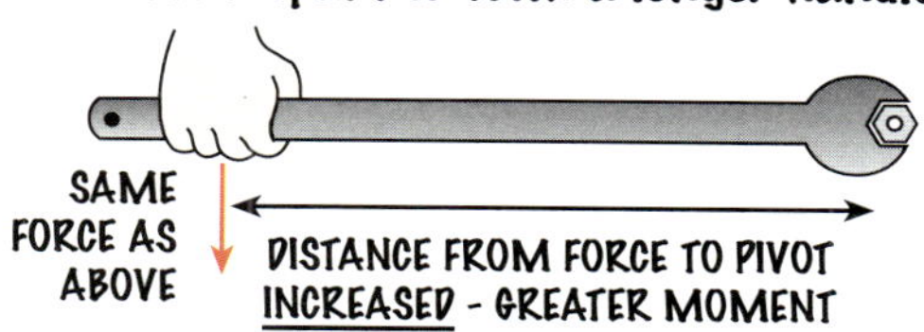

2. INCREASE FORCE APPLIED ...

... push harder or get your Dad to do it.

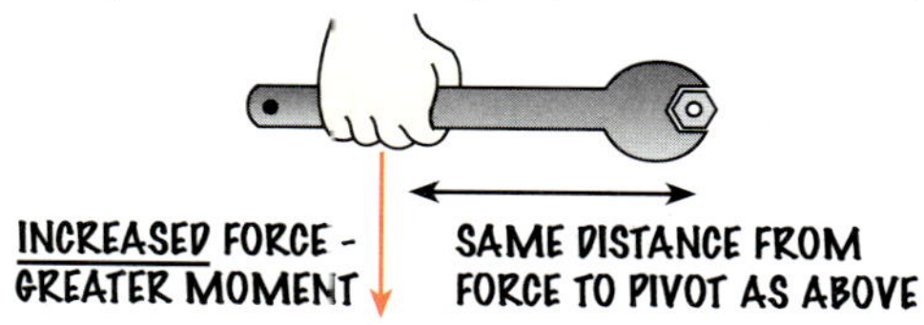

The moment of a force is given by the relationship:

MOMENT = FORCE x DISTANCE FROM PIVOT

The moment of a force is measured in ...

- Newton centimetre (Ncm).
- Newton metre (Nm).

EXAMPLE

The boy above exerts a force of 80N and the distance from his hand to the pivot is 10cm. What moment does he exert?

Using our relationship: MOMENT = FORCE x DISTANCE FORM PIVOT

= 80N x 10cm = 800Ncm

PRINCIPLE OF MOMENTS

The seesaw below has TWO children on it, one either side.

THE BOY EXERTS AN ANTI-CLOCKWISE MOMENT EQUAL TO ... HIS WEIGHT x DISTANCE FROM PIVOT

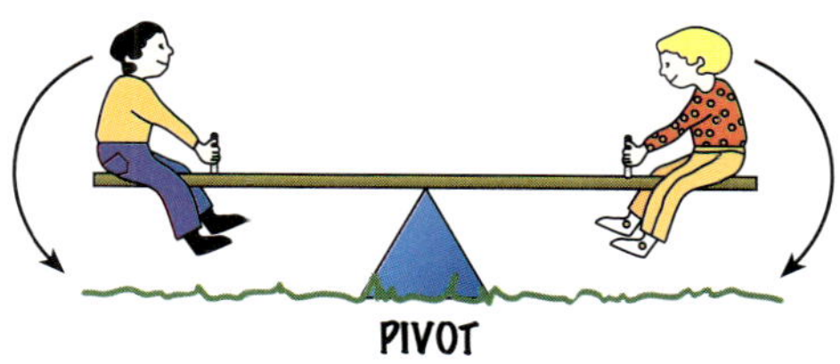

THE GIRL EXERTS A CLOCKWISE MOMENT EQUAL TO ... HER WEIGHT x DISTANCE FROM PIVOT

- EACH CHILD EXERTS A MOMENT ABOUT THE PIVOT ...
- ... and if these TWO MOMENTS ARE EQUAL then the seesaw is BALANCED.

This is known as the PRINCIPLE OF MOMENTS.

NB. WEIGHT IS THE FORCE DUE TO GRAVITY (see page 58)

When balanced ... **TOTAL CLOCKWISE MOMENT = TOTAL ANTI-CLOCKWISE MOMENT**

EXAMPLE

The girl in the diagram above weighs 250N and she is 2 metres from the pivot. Where must the boy who weighs 300N sit in order for the seesaw to be balanced?

When balanced, TOTAL C.M = TOTAL A-C.M. ∴ 250N x 2m = 300N x DISTANCE

$\therefore$ DISTANCE = $\frac{250 \times 2}{300}$ = 1.6m

1. What is a MOMENT and what are the TWO ways of increasing the moment? 2. What is the PRINCIPLE OF MOMENTS?
2. Repeat the example just above where the girl now sits 3 metres from the pivot.

MEASURING SPEED

One way of describing the movement of an object is by measuring its SPEED.

- Consider a cyclist travelling at 8 metres per second (8m/s).

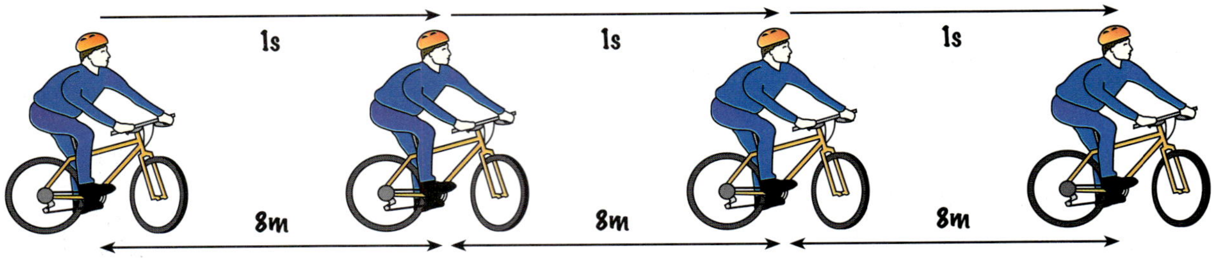

- The cyclist travels a DISTANCE of 8 METRES ...
- ... <u>EVERY</u> 1 SECOND.

And so ...

- In order to work out the SPEED of ANY MOVING OBJECT ...
- ... we need to KNOW TWO THINGS.

> 1. THE DISTANCE IT TRAVELS and ...
> 2. HOW LONG IT TAKES TO TRAVEL THAT DISTANCE.

We can then use this relationship:

$$\text{SPEED} = \frac{\text{DISTANCE TRAVELLED}}{\text{TIME TAKEN}}$$

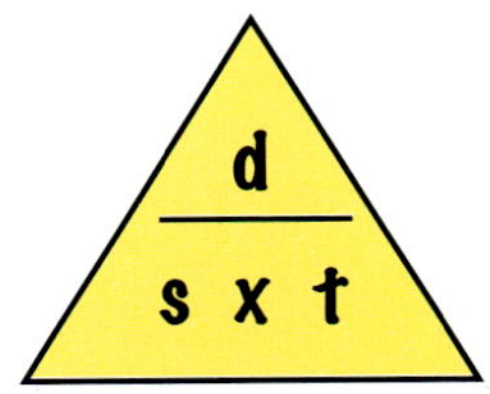

THIS IS A FORMULA TRIANGLE

- Speed is measured in ...
  - Metres per second (m/s).
  - Kilometres per hour (km/h).
  - Miles per hour (miles/h).

EXAMPLES

1. Calculate the speed of a cyclist who travels 200 metres in 40 seconds.

Using our relationship: $\text{SPEED} = \frac{\text{DISTANCE TRAVELLED}}{\text{TIME TAKEN}} = \frac{200\text{m}}{40\text{s}} = 5 \text{ m/s}.$

2. The cyclist then carries on at this speed for 2 minutes. What distance will the cyclist travel?

Time given is in MINUTES, and we need it in SECONDS because the SPEED is in metres per SECOND ...

... and so, 2 minutes = 2 x 60 seconds = 120s.

Using our relationship: (which is rearranged using formula triangle)

DISTANCE TRAVELLED = SPEED x TIME TAKEN

= 5m/s x 120s

DISTANCE TRAVELLED = 600m

3. A car on the motorway travels 10 Kilometres in 6 minutes. What was it's speed in Km/h?

Time given is in MINUTES, and we need it in HOURS because the SPEED needs to be in Km per HOUR ...

... and so, 6 minutes = $\frac{6}{60}$ hours = 0.1 hour.

Using our relationship: $\text{SPEED} = \frac{\text{DISTANCE TRAVELLED}}{\text{TIME TAKEN}} = \frac{10\text{Km}}{0.1\text{h}} = 100\text{Km/h}.$

1. What is SPEED? Write out the formula and the formula triangle.
2. An athlete runs 400 metres in 50 seconds. What is the speed of the athlete?
3. If the athlete could carry on at this speed for another 3 minutes, how far would the athlete run?
4. A motorbike travels at 60Km/h for 40 minutes. What distance does the motorbike travel?

ENERGY exists in many FORMS. These are the most common ones:

LIGHT

- Energy given out by ANY HOT OBJECT (and some cold ones).
- We need light to SEE and plants use it for PHOTOSYNTHESIS.
- The SUN and LIGHT BULBS give out light energy.

SOUND

- Energy created by ANY VIBRATING OBJECT.
- We use sound to communicate with each other.
- Our VOCAL CHORDS and LOUDSPEAKERS create sound energy.

ELECTRICAL

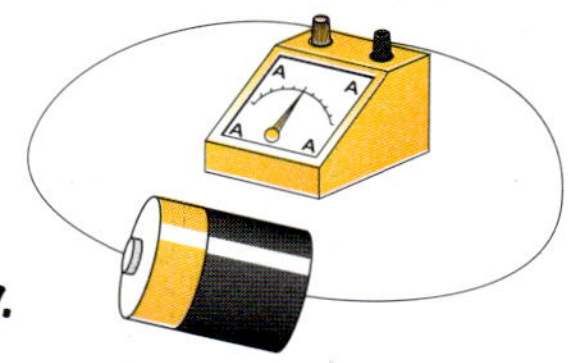

- Our most convenient form of energy.
- Nearly all appliances in the home need electrical energy to work.
- A BATTERY and a GENERATOR (in a POWER STATION) are sources of electrical energy.

THERMAL (or HEAT)

- The thermal energy contained in any WARM or HOT OBJECT depends on ...
- ... the TEMPERATURE AND SIZE of the object.
- BURNING COAL and HOT WATER contain thermal energy.

KINETIC (or MOVEMENT)

- The energy an object has because it is MOVING.
- The FASTER it moves the greater its kinetic energy.
- A RUNNER or a MOVING CAR has kinetic energy.

CHEMICAL POTENTIAL

- Energy contained in FOOD or any FUEL (or even a battery come to that!)
- The energy in FOOD is RELEASED when we respire in our cells, ...
- ... and the energy in FUEL is RELEASED when it is burned.

GRAVITATIONAL POTENTIAL

- The energy an object has due to its height above the earth's surface.
- The HIGHER UP it is, the greater its potential energy (due to earth's gravitational pull).
- A SKIER at the top of a mountain has gravitational potential energy.

ELASTIC POTENTIAL

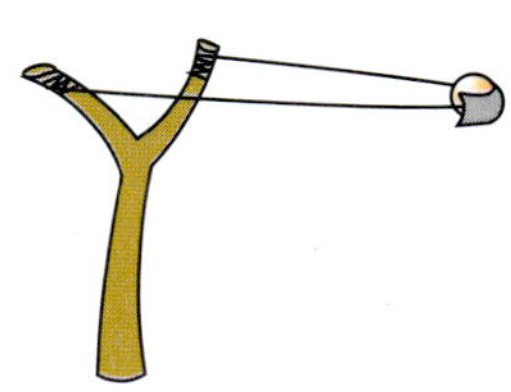

- This is the energy stored due to stretching or compressing an object ...
- ... which has the ability to regain its original shape and size (i.e. is ELASTIC).
- Springs, catapults and longbows can store elastic potential energy.

1. Write out the EIGHT forms of energy above. For each one explain what that energy is.
2. Which energy or energies does a) a burning candle give out b) water have at the top of a waterfall and c) a cyclist have that is moving?

NON-RENEWABLES

- These will ONE DAY RUN OUT and ONCE USED they CANNOT BE USED AGAIN.
- OIL, GAS and COAL can be used to GENERATE ELECTRICITY when ...
- ... they are burned to produce HEAT which boils water to make STEAM ...
- ... to drive the TURBINES which turn the GENERATORS producing ELECTRICITY.

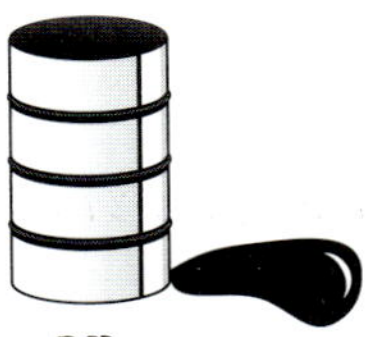

OIL

Formed from ...

- ... the REMAINS of PLANT ...
- ... and ANIMAL LIFE.

GAS

Formed from ...

- ... the REMAINS of PLANT ...
- ... and ANIMAL LIFE.

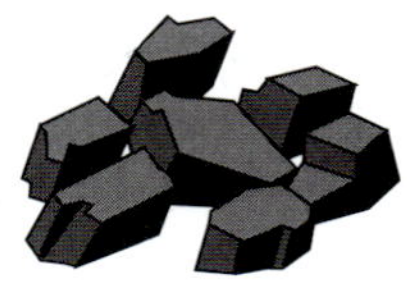

COAL

Formed from ...

- ... the REMAINS of PLANTS ...
- ... and TREES.

THE SUN

- THE ORIGINAL SOURCE OF ...
- ... MOST ENERGY RESOURCES.
- PLANTS STORE THE SUN'S ENERGY ...
- ... DURING PHOTOSYNTHESIS.
- ANIMALS THEN EAT ...
- ... THE PLANTS.

RENEWABLES

BIOMASS

- PLANTS and TREES, via PHOTOSYNTHESIS can provide FUEL for HEATING.

FOOD

- CROPS photosynthesise, grow and can be harvested to provide FOOD supplies.

WIND

- Created by the HEATING effect of the SUN.

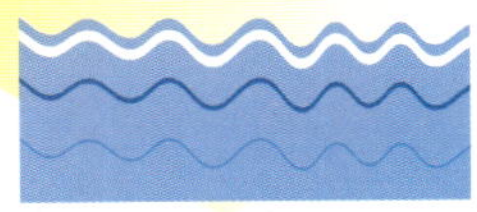

WAVES

- Created partly due to the WIND.

- These will NOT RUN OUT and are CONTINUALLY BEING REPLACED.
- WIND and WAVES can be used to drive TURBINES directly for the production of electricity.
- Other renewable energy resources are SOLAR, HYDRO-ELECTRIC and TIDAL.

BATTERIES

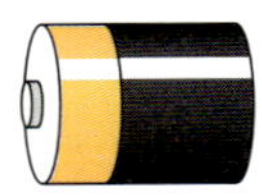

- These contain CHEMICAL ENERGY which can be converted into ELECTRICAL ENERGY.
- They are convenient to use although they do eventually "go flat".
- They are an ideal way of storing energy which has been produced from any of the resources above.

1. What are NON-RENEWABLE energy resources? Give 3 examples and explain how they can be used to generate electricity.
2. What are RENEWABLE energy resources? Give 4 examples and explain how they can be used to provide us with energy.
3. What is a battery? Why do they eventually go flat?

CONSERVATION OF ENERGY

Whenever ...
- Energy is transferred from ONE FORM to ANOTHER ...
- ... some is 'WASTED' - usually as heat and often sound ...
- ... which just spreads out and can't be used again.

Although ...
- The AMOUNT of energy measured in JOULES (J) to begin with ...
- ... is always CONSERVED which means ...
- ... there is still the SAME AMOUNT OF ENERGY ...
- ... BEFORE and AFTER the transfer.

ENERGY TRANSFER DEVICES

Here are FOUR everyday examples of the intended (useful) energy transfer and wastage in everyday devices.

1. TUNGSTEN FILAMENT LIGHT BULB

2. LOW ENERGY LIGHT BULB

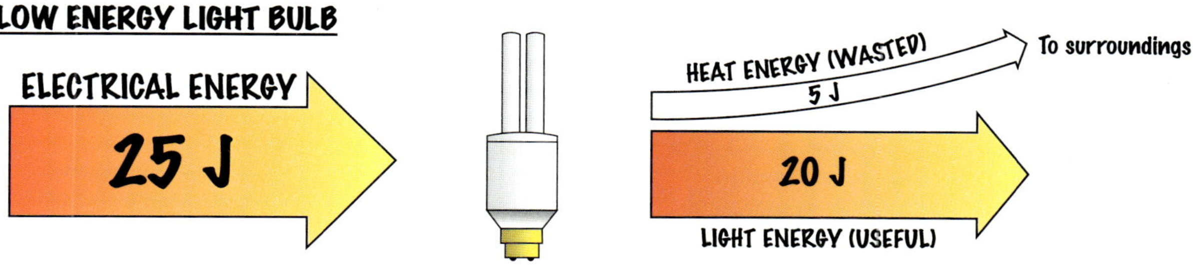

3. ELECTRIC KETTLE

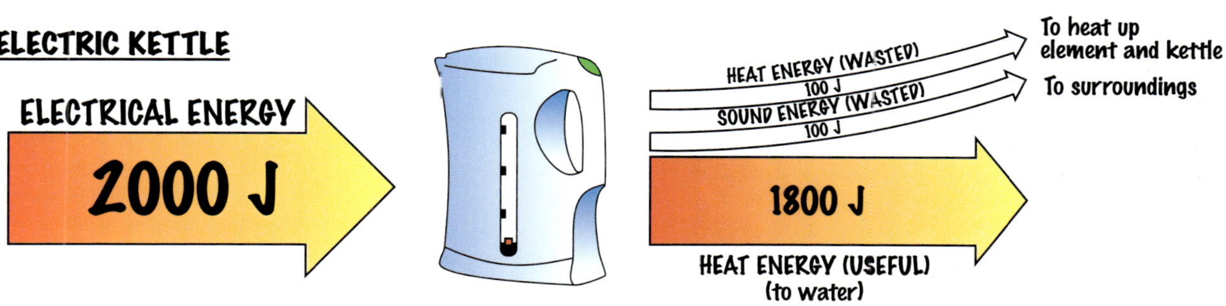

4. VACUUM CLEANER

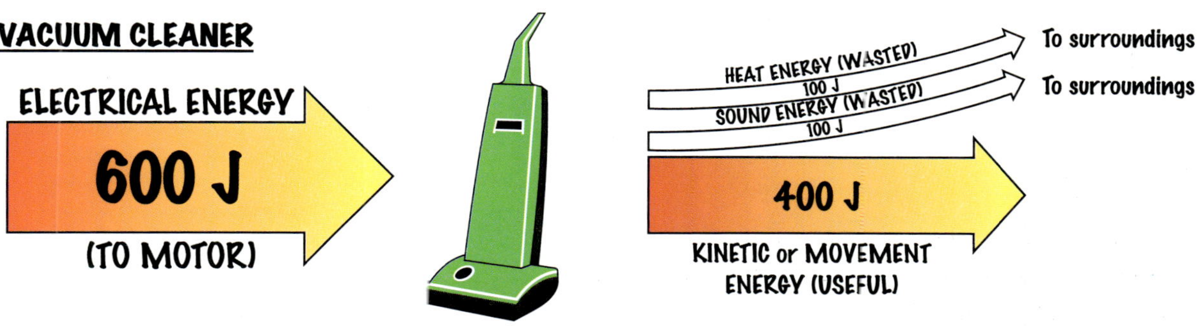

1. When energy is TRANSFERRED from one form to another why is some always WASTED and what happens to it?
2. What is energy measured in and when there is a transfer of energy why can we say that energy is CONSERVED?
3. Which of the above appliances is the a) LEAST and b) MOST WASTEFUL? Explain why?

LIGHT

- LIGHT is a FORM of ENERGY (see page 63) ...
- ... that travels at an incredibly high speed (300,000,000 m/s if you really want to know!) ...
- ... and is DETECTED using our EYES.

HOW SHADOWS ARE FORMED

- SHADOWS are formed because ...
- ... LIGHT TRAVELS IN STRAIGHT LINES and ...
- ... is UNABLE TO PASS THROUGH SOME MATERIALS OR OBJECTS.

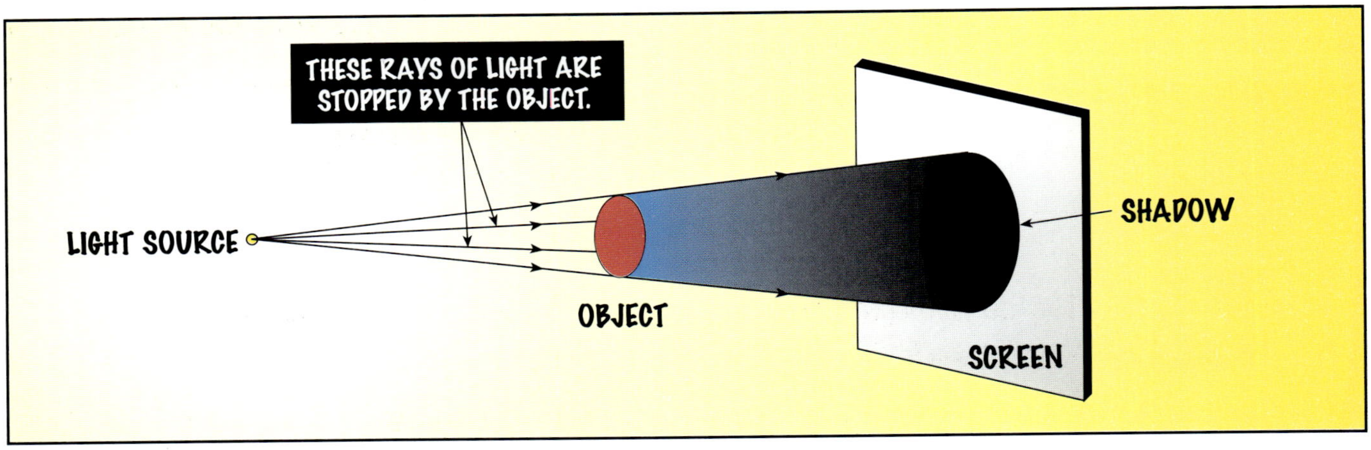

Shadows can be made bigger by ...

1. INCREASING THE DISTANCE BETWEEN THE OBJECT AND THE SCREEN.
2. DECREASING THE DISTANCE BETWEEN THE LIGHT SOURCE AND THE OBJECT.

WHY WE SEE THINGS

- We can SEE LUMINOUS SOURCES e.g. LIGHT BULBS, SUN, STARS, CANDLES because ... ... the LIGHT THEY GIVE OUT ENTERS OUR EYES.
- We can also SEE NON-LUMINOUS OBJECTS e.g. THIS PAGE, OBJECTS AROUND YOU because ... ... LIGHT FROM A LUMINOUS SOURCE IS REFLECTED OFF THEM INTO OUR EYES.

1. What is LIGHT?
2. Draw a fully labelled diagram to show how a shadow is formed. What are the TWO ways that the shadow can be made bigger?
3. What is a LUMINOUS SOURCE and a NON-LUMINOUS OBJECT? Explain how we can see either.

REFLECTION AND REFRACTION OF LIGHT

REFLECTION OF LIGHT

- Most surfaces **REFLECT LIGHT** although ...
- ... **MIRRORS** and **POLISHED METALS** are the best reflectors.

Let's look at the reflection of a ray of light by a plane (flat) mirror ...

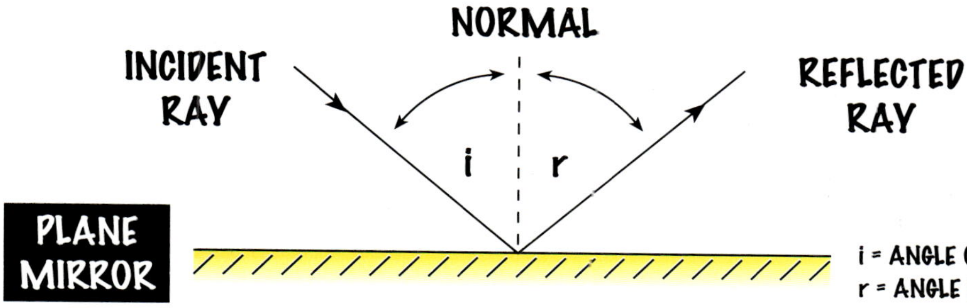

i = ANGLE OF INCIDENCE
r = ANGLE OF REFLECTION

Diffuse reflection occurs when light strikes an irregular surface.

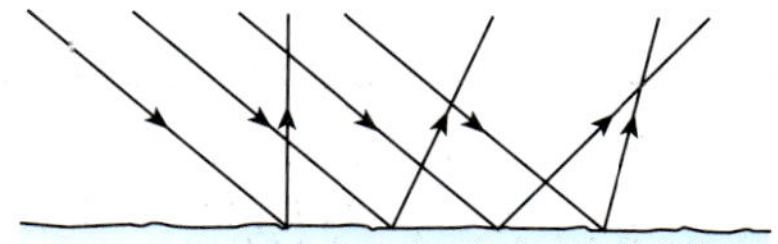

e.g. paper-no clear reflection is seen.

ANGLE OF INCIDENCE = ANGLE OF REFLECTION

Very often you will get asked to complete a diagram to show how a mirror reflects a ray of light. You will need a **RULER** and a **PROTRACTOR**.

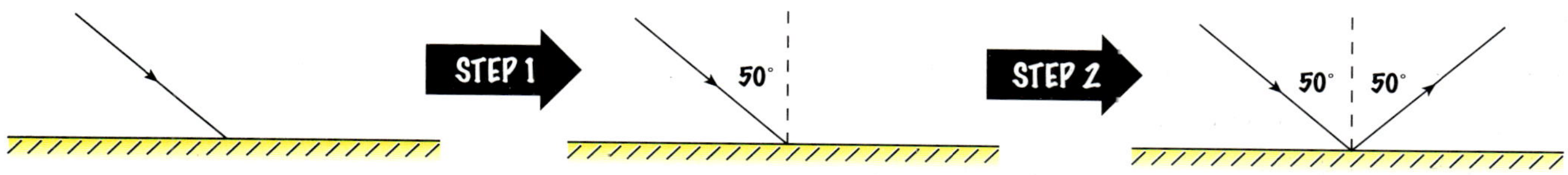

- COMPLETE THE FOLLOWING DIAGRAM.

- DRAW IN THE NORMAL ...
- ...dotted line at 90° to the mirror.
- MEASURE ANGLE OF INCIDENCE ...
- ... using a protractor and ...
- .. mark it on your diagram.

- MEASURE OUT THE ANGLE OF REFLECTION ...
- ... it must be the same as the angle of incidence ...
- ... and mark it on your diagram.
- DRAW IN THE REFLECTED RAY ...
- ... with an arrow to show its direction.

REFRACTION OF LIGHT

- Light **CHANGES DIRECTION** when it **CROSSES A BOUNDARY** ...
- ... between **ONE TRANSPARENT MATERIAL (MEDIUM) AND ANOTHER** providing ...
- ... they are **DIFFERENT MATERIALS** ...
- ... unless it meets the boundary at 90° **(ALONG THE NORMAL)**.

Let's look at a ray of light passing through a glass block.

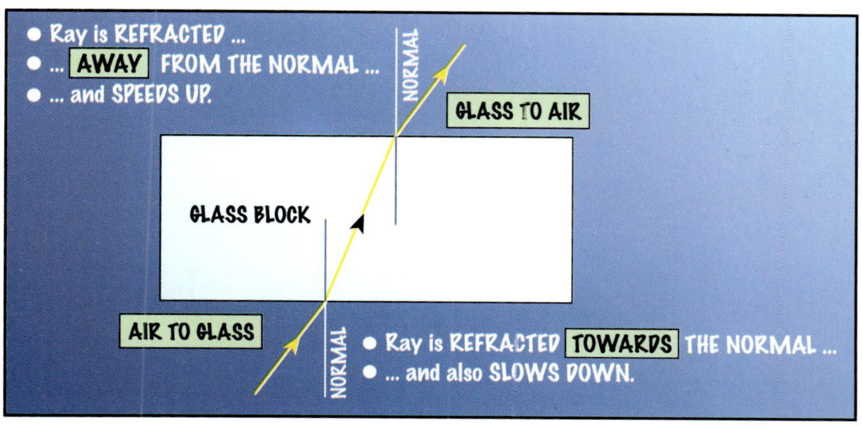

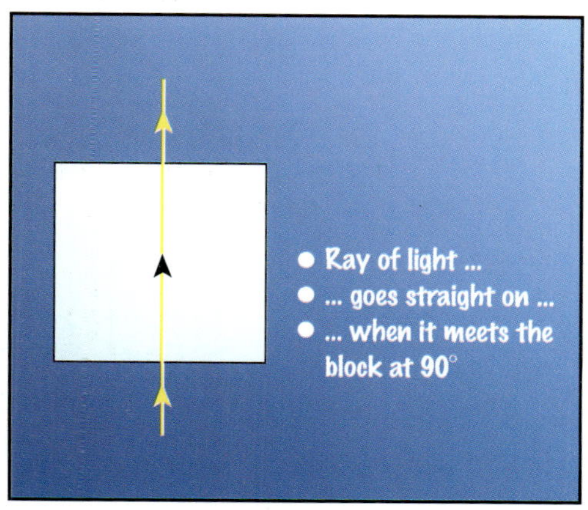

1. Draw a fully labelled diagram to show the reflection of light from a **PLANE MIRROR**.
2. Draw a plane mirror and then **ANY INCIDENT RAY** onto the mirror. Complete the diagram to show how the mirror reflects the ray (make sure you use a ruler and protractor). 3. What is **REFRACTION**? Draw a diagram to show a ray of light passing through a **GLASS BLOCK** (the ray of light does not meet the block at 90°).

THE RAINBOW EFFECT

- When WHITE LIGHT passes ...
- ... through a GLASS PRISM ...
- ... it SPLITS UP into ...
- ... a RANGE OF COLOURS ...
- ... RED, ORANGE, YELLOW, GREEN, BLUE, INDIGO, VIOLET ...
- ... called a SPECTRUM.

- The effect is known as **DISPERSION.** Red light is deviated (bent) the least and violet the most.

COLOURED FILTERS

- These ALLOW some COLOURS to PASS THROUGH while ...
- ... OTHER COLOURS are ABSORBED by the filter.

Very simply:

- THE COLOUR OF THE FILTER ...
  - ... IS THE COLOUR OF THE LIGHT THAT PASSES THROUGH.

Some Examples

1.

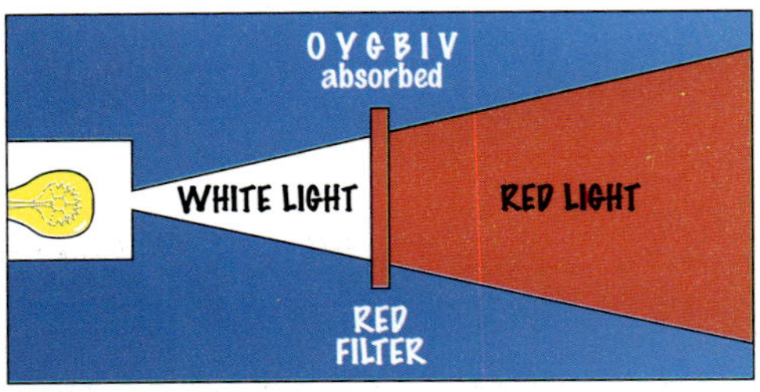

2.

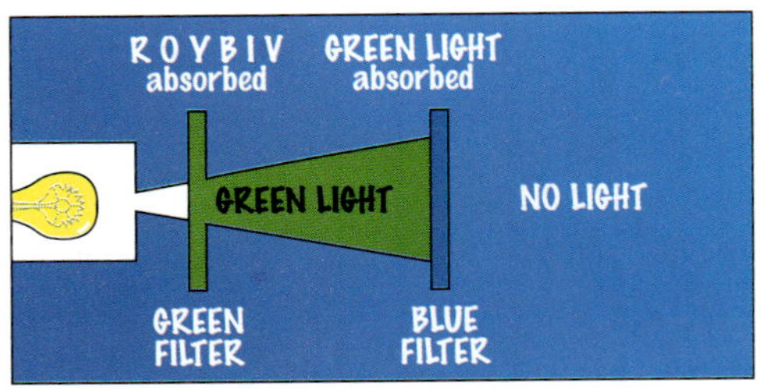

COLOURED OBJECTS

- The COLOUR of an OBJECT is the COLOUR OF THE LIGHT IT REFLECTS.
- ALL the OTHER COLOURS are ABSORBED by the object.
- WHITE OBJECTS REFLECT ALL COLOURS AND ABSORB NONE while ...
- ... BLACK OBJECTS ABSORB ALL COLOURS AND REFLECT NONE!

Example

Nicola is going to the disco. She's wearing a BLUE top with RED spots and GREEN trousers (very trendy). She spends her time on the dance floor ...

- Her top is still BLUE ...
- ... with RED spots.
- Trousers still GREEN.

- Her top is now completely BLACK.
- Her Trousers are still GREEN.

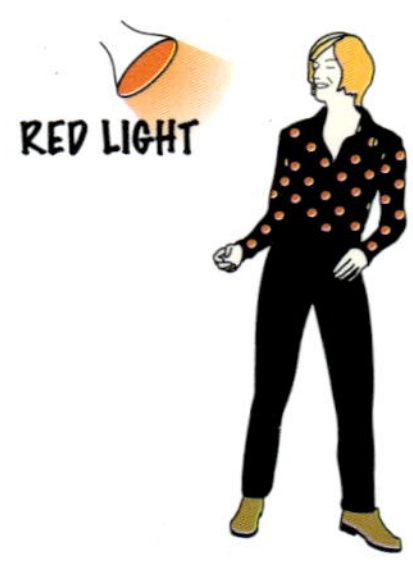

- Her top is now BLACK ...
- ... with RED SPOTS.
- Her Trousers are now BLACK.

1. What is DISPERSION? Draw a diagram to show how a glass prism can split up white light into a spectrum.
2. Draw diagrams to show what happens if a) white light is shone on to a BLUE FILTER b) if white light is shone on to a RED FILTER followed by a GREEN FILTER.
3. How would the girl just above look if BLUE light was shone onto her?

SOUND

- SOUND is a FORM of ENERGY (see page 63) ...
- ... that is PRODUCED when something VIBRATES BACKWARDS and FORWARDS.
- Sound TRAVELS much more SLOWLY than LIGHT, ...
- ... this is why we get the LIGHTNING FIRST and THEN the THUNDER.
- Sound needs a MATERIAL e.g. air, water, wood to TRAVEL THROUGH as ...
- ... it CANNOT travel through a VACUUM (EMPTY SPACE).

HEARING SOUND

WE HEAR BECAUSE SOUND MAKES THE EAR DRUM VIBRATE. → As long as ... → .. THE SOUND IS WITHIN THE FREQUENCY RANGE OUR EARS CAN DETECT. THIS RANGE DECREASES AS WE GET OLDER. → However ... → ... LOUD SOUNDS CAN CAUSE DAMAGE TO THE EAR DRUM, EVEN DEAFNESS.

PITCH AND LOUDNESS OF SOUND

The sound produced by a vibrating object can change in TWO ways ...

1. PITCH and ... 2. LOUDNESS.

Let's consider a simple musical instrument, a GUITAR.

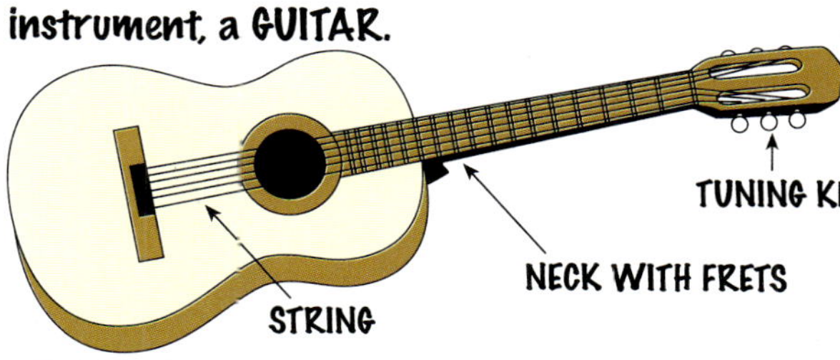

There are THREE ways that the PITCH of the sound produced by a guitar STRING can be changed ...

1. CHANGE THICKNESS OF STRING ...	• a THINNER STRING is HIGHER PITCHED. • Most guitars have six strings of different thicknesses.
2. CHANGE LENGTH OF STRING ...	• a SHORTER STRING is HIGHER PITCHED. • The guitar neck has frets on it.
3. CHANGE TIGHTNESS OF STRING ...	• a TIGHTER STRING is HIGHER PITCHED. • The guitar has tuning keys at the end of the neck.

... and ONE way that the LOUDNESS of the sound produced by a guitar STRING can be changed ...

PLUCK THE STRING HARDER ...	• The harder you pluck, the LOUDER the sound.

FREQUENCY AND AMPLITUDE OF SOUND

FREQUENCY

This is the NUMBER of VIBRATIONS PRODUCED in ONE SECOND.

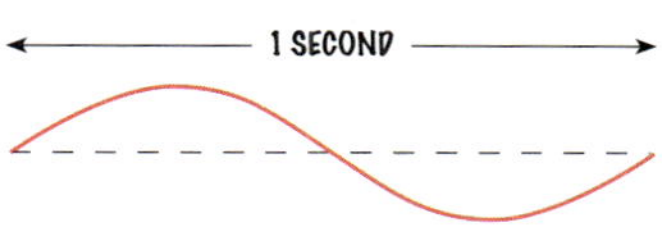

ONE COMPLETE VIBRATION ...
... IN ONE SECOND.
A LOW FREQUENCY MEANS ...
... THE SOUND IS LOW PITCH.

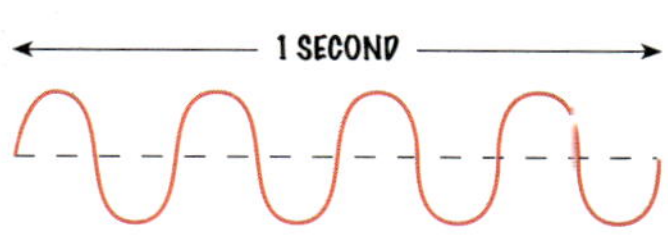

FOUR COMPLETE VIBRATIONS ...
... IN ONE SECOND.
A HIGHER FREQUENCY MEANS ...
... THE SOUND IS HIGHER PITCHED.

AMPLITUDE

This is the GREATEST SIZE of the VIBRATION.

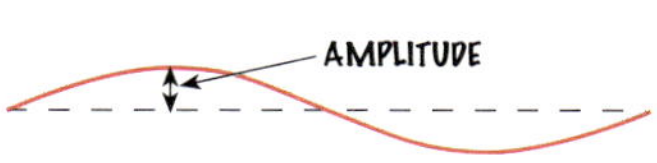

A LOW AMPLITUDE MEANS ...
... THE SOUND IS QUIET.

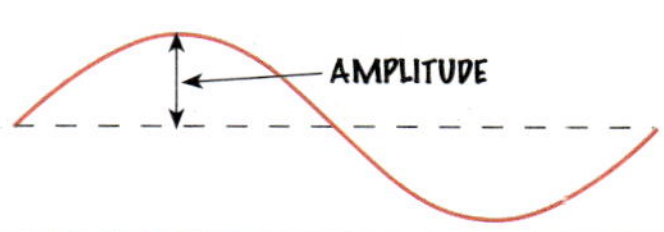

A BIGGER AMPLITUDE MEANS ...
... THE SOUND IS LOUDER.

1. What is SOUND and how is it produced?
2. Apart from thunder and lightning give TWO other examples which prove that sound travels slower than light?
3. For a guitar what are the a) 3 ways that the PITCH of the sound and b) the 1 WAY that the LOUDNESS of the sound can be changed?

The SOLAR SYSTEM is made up of ...

- ... the SUN which is in the middle ...
- ... surrounded by 9 DIFFERENT PLANETS.
- These planets move around the sun in paths called ORBITS ...
- ... which are SLIGHTLY SQUASHED CIRCLES.

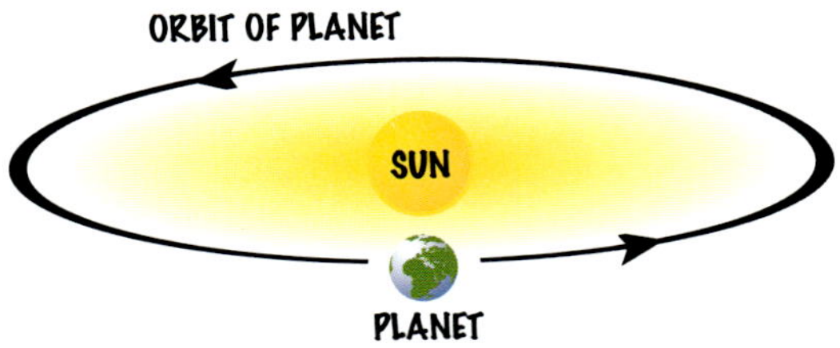

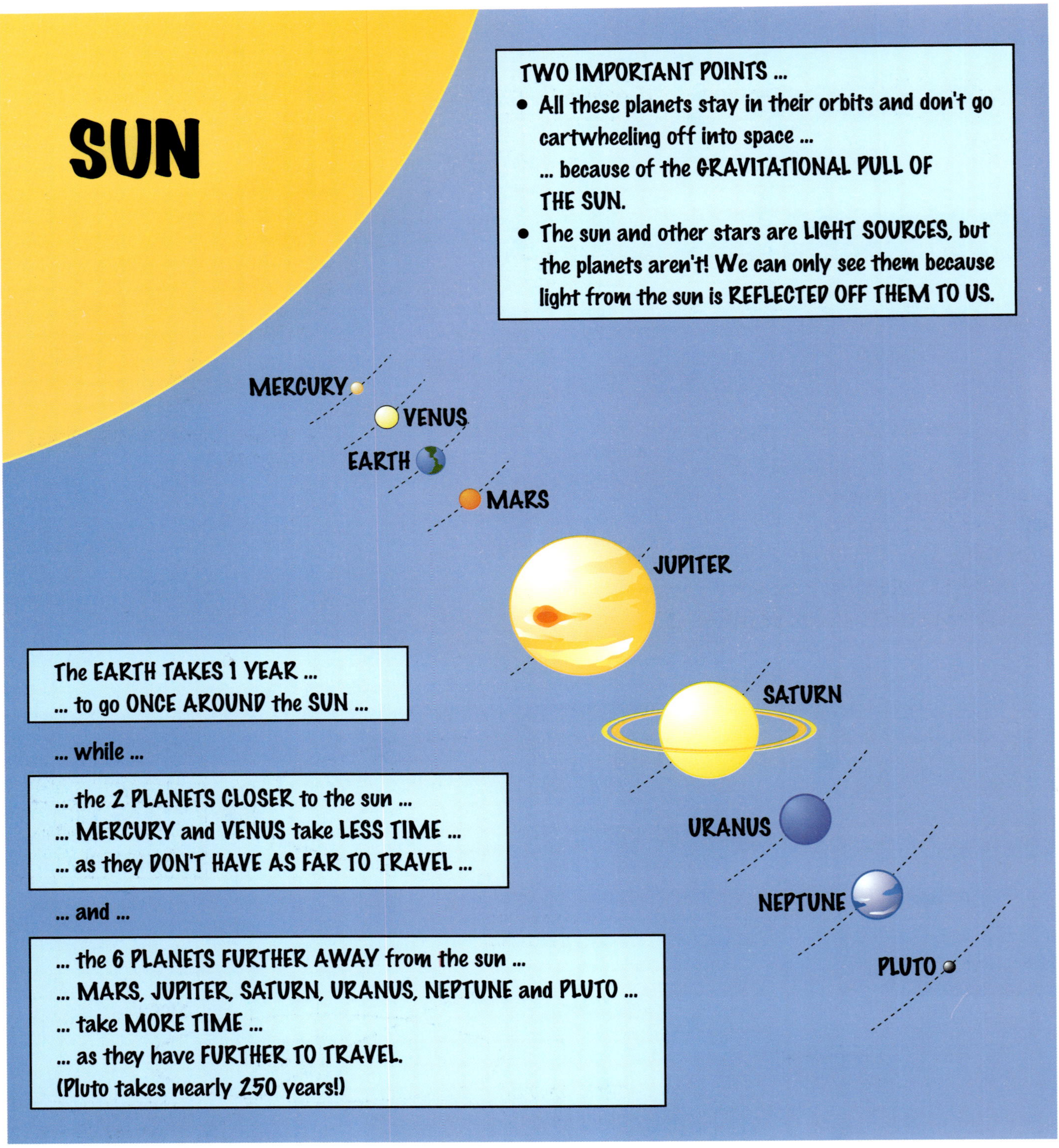

TWO IMPORTANT POINTS ...

- All these planets stay in their orbits and don't go cartwheeling off into space ... ... because of the GRAVITATIONAL PULL OF THE SUN.
- The sun and other stars are LIGHT SOURCES, but the planets aren't! We can only see them because light from the sun is REFLECTED OFF THEM TO US.

The EARTH TAKES 1 YEAR ...
... to go ONCE AROUND the SUN ...

... while ...

... the 2 PLANETS CLOSER to the sun ...
... MERCURY and VENUS take LESS TIME ...
... as they DON'T HAVE AS FAR TO TRAVEL ...

... and ...

... the 6 PLANETS FURTHER AWAY from the sun ...
... MARS, JUPITER, SATURN, URANUS, NEPTUNE and PLUTO ...
... take MORE TIME ...
... as they have FURTHER TO TRAVEL.
(Pluto takes nearly 250 years!)

1. What are the NINE planets that make up the solar system? List them in order FROM the sun.
2. How is it possible for us to see these planets and why can we not see them at certain times of the year?
3. Which planets take a) LESS and b) MORE time to orbit the Sun than the Earth? Why is this?

THE EARTH

The Earth ...

- ... SPINS AROUND on an imaginary TILTED AXIS ...
- ... completing ONE ROTATION ...
- ... every 24 HOURS ...
- ... giving us DAY TIME and NIGHT TIME

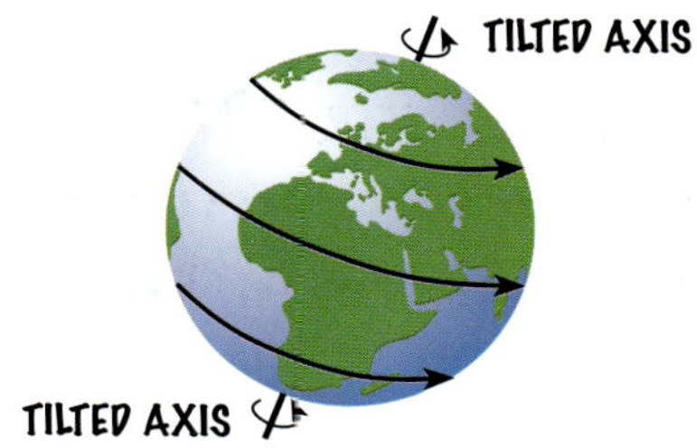

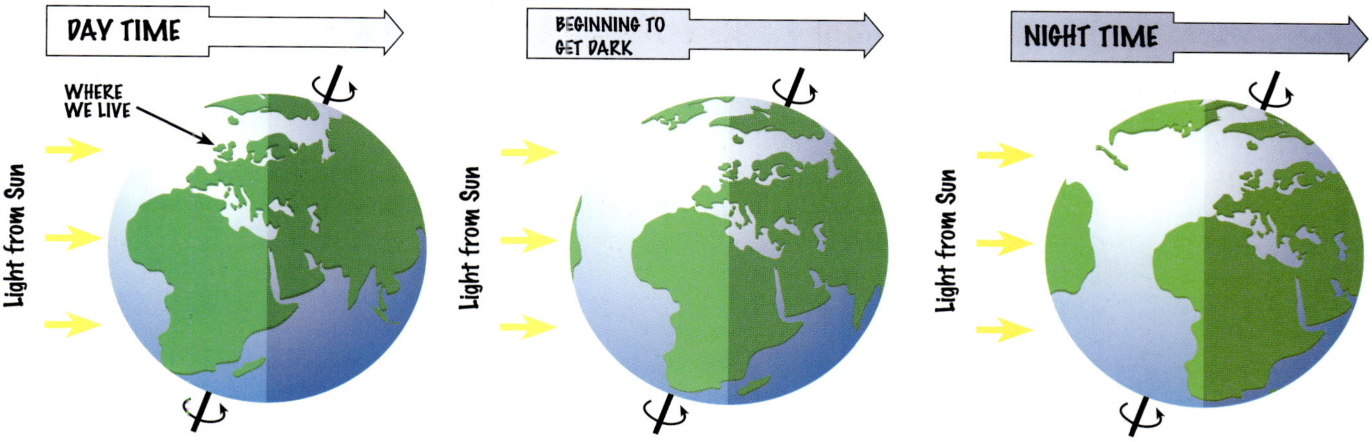

- We are FACING TOWARDS THE SUN.

- We are FACING AWAY FROM THE SUN.

THE FOUR SEASONS

The Earth ...

- ... ORBITS THE SUN ONCE every 365 ¼ DAYS (a YEAR) ...
- ... giving us the FOUR DIFFERENT SEASONS.

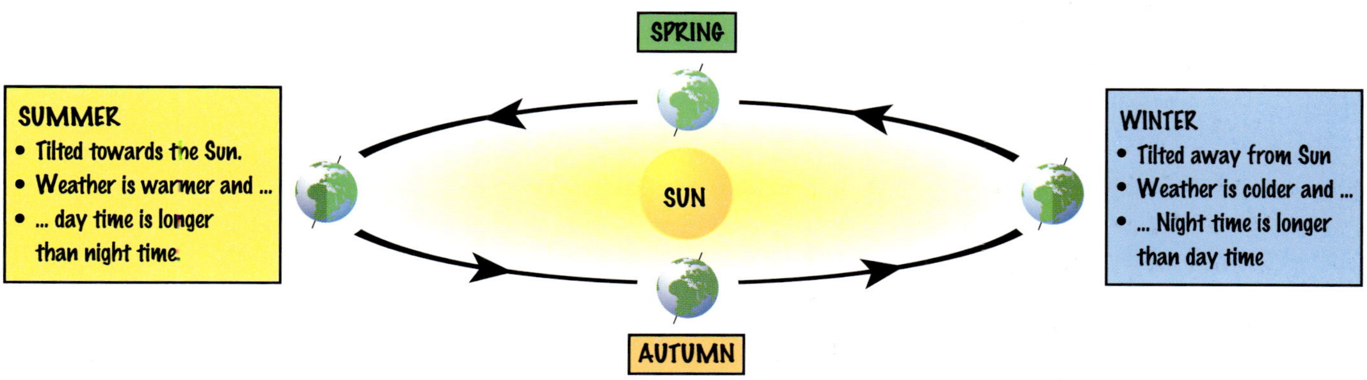

THE MOON

The Moon ...

- ... ORBITS THE EARTH ONCE ...
- ... every 28 DAYS.

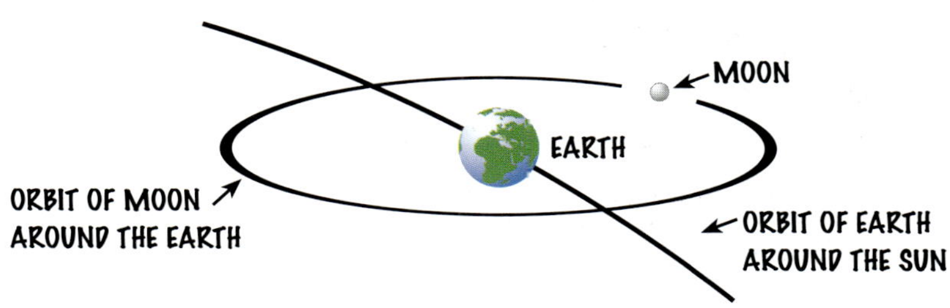

1. Why do we get DAY TIME and NIGHT TIME?
2. How long does it take the Earth to orbit the Sun? Why do we get the different seasons?
3. How long does it take for the Moon to orbit the Earth? The Moon does not give out light so why can we see it?

APPARENT MOVEMENT OF THE SUN AND STARS

During DAYTIME ...
- the SUN appears to move across the sky ...

... while at NIGHT-TIME
- the STARS appear to move across the sky.

However ...
- Both the SUN and the STARS ARE NOT MOVING AT ALL! ...
- ... and this APPARENT MOVEMENT across the sky is created ...
- ... because the EARTH is constantly ROTATING about its axis.

APPARENT MOVEMENT OF THE SUN

- At DAYTIME the APPARENT MOVEMENT of the SUN ...
- ... is a CURVED PATH across the sky where ...
- ... it RISES in the EAST and SETS in the WEST.
- This apparent movement of the sun changes ...
- ... as the EARTH ORBITS the SUN giving us the different seasons.

SUMMER

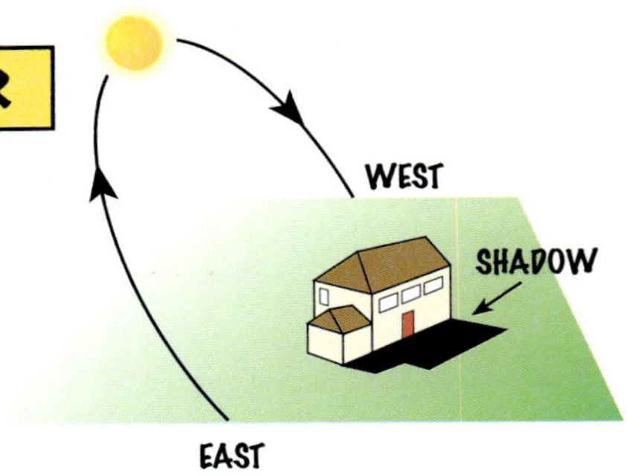

WINTER

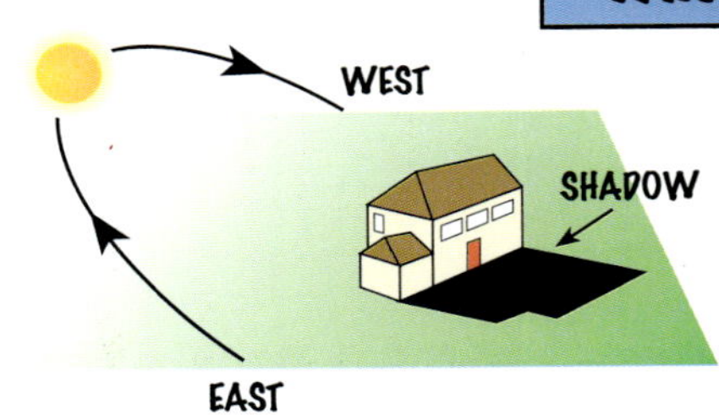

During the SUMMER ...
- ... we are TILTED TOWARDS THE SUN. This means ...
- ... the SUN is HIGHER in the SKY and ...
- ... DAYTIME is LONGER than NIGHT-TIME ...
- ... giving us warm, sunny days.
- LENGTH of SHADOW formed by sun ...
- ... is SHORTER than at winter time.

During the WINTER ...
- ... we are TILTED AWAY FROM THE SUN. This means ...
- ... the SUN is LOWER in the SKY and ...
- ... DAYTIME is SHORTER than NIGHT-TIME ...
- ... giving us colder days.
- LENGTH of SHADOW formed by sun ...
- ... is LONGER than at summertime.

APPARENT MOVEMENT OF THE STARS

- At NIGHTIME the APPARENT MOVEMENT of the STARS ...
- ... are CURVED PATHS across the sky.

1. Why is the movement of the SUN and STARS APPARENT?
2. Draw diagrams to show the movement of the Sun during a) summer and b) winter. Why does length of shadow change?
3. Why is there NO apparent movement of the 'POLE' STAR?
4. The night sky just above represents a total length of time of a) 1 hour b) 6 hours or c) 12 hours? Explain your answer.

A SATELLITE ...

- ... is a SMALL OBJECT ...
- ... WHICH IS IN ORBIT AROUND a MUCH LARGER OBJECT.
- The EARTH and the other PLANETS are NATURAL SATELLITES of the SUN while ...
- ... the MOON is a NATURAL SATELLITE of the EARTH.

However ...

- ... there are ARTIFICIAL SATELLITES in orbit AROUND THE EARTH.
- These have been put into orbit BY US ...
- ... and each one has a SPECIFIC JOB TO DO.

1. MONITORING THE WEATHER

- These collect INFORMATION about the ATMOSPHERE including MOVEMENT OF CLOUDS ...
- ... so that WEATHER FORECASTS can be made.

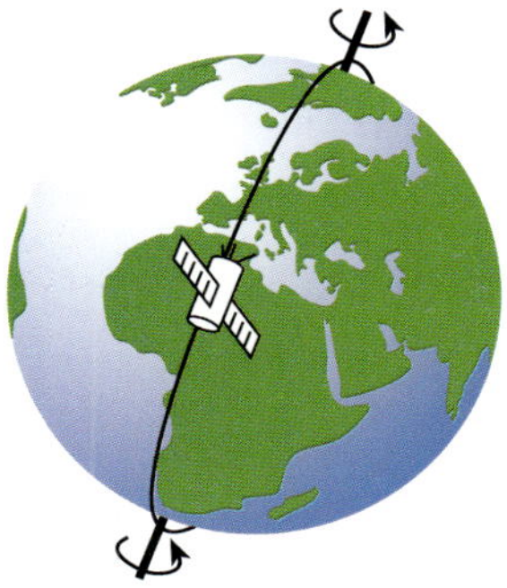

THE SATELLITE HAS AN ORBIT WHICH PASSES CONTINUOUSLY OVER THE NORTH AND SOUTH POLE. THESE SATELLITES ORBIT THE EARTH SEVERAL TIMES EVERY DAY.

2. OBSERVATION OF THE EARTH

- These take PHOTOGRAPHS of any 'DISASTERS' which may be happening ...
- ... floods, earthquakes, volcano eruptions, crop failures.
- They can also be used for 'SPYING' purposes!

3. COMMUNICATION

- These LINK UP different COUNTRIES, often in different continents so that ...
- ... RADIO, TV broadcasts and TELEPHONE calls can be SENT from ONE COUNTRY TO ANOTHER.

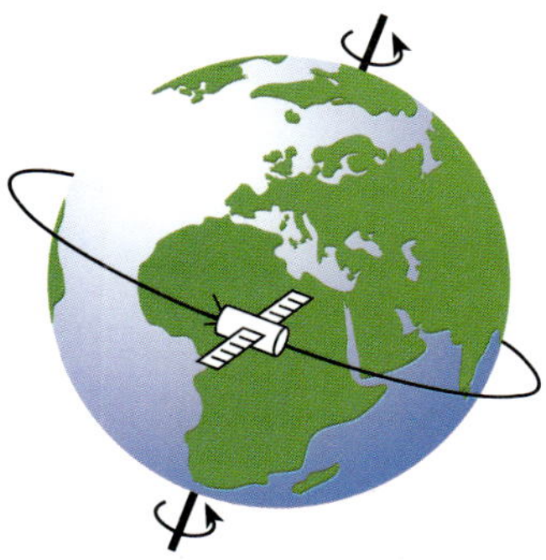

THE SATELLITE HAS AN ORBIT PASSING OVER THE EQUATOR WHICH TAKES 24 HOURS TO COMPLETE. THIS MEANS THAT IT ALWAYS STAYS AT THE SAME POINT ABOVE THE EQUATOR.

4. EXPLORATION OF THE SOLAR SYSTEM

- These are in orbit ABOVE THE EARTH'S ATMOSPHERE.
- These have TELESCOPES and the SOLAR SYSTEM and beyond can be OBSERVED without ...
- ... any INTERFERENCE from the ATMOSPHERE, CLOUDS and WEATHER STORMS.

1. What is a SATELLITE?
2. What are NATURAL satellites? Give FIVE examples.
3. What are ARTIFICIAL satellites? Explain using diagrams how artificial satellites are used for a) monitoring the weather b) communication and c) exploration of the solar system.

1 Draw circuit diagrams for each of the following circuits.

2 Below are two circuits, one series and the other parallel. Each circuit has ONE ammeter reading given.

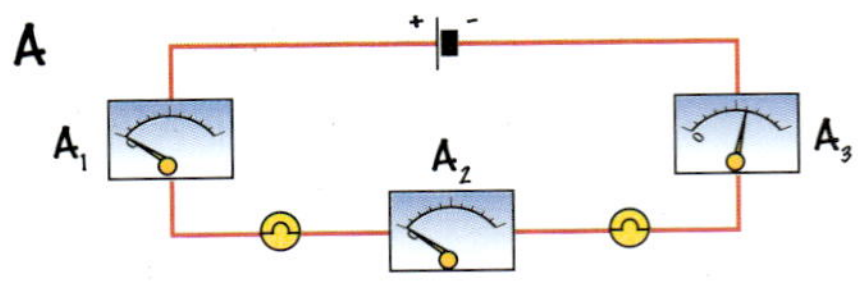

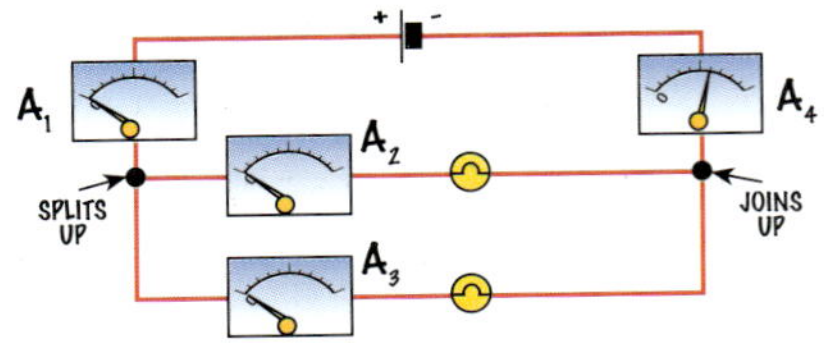

a) Copy and complete diagram A showing the other ammeter readings.

b) Copy and complete diagram B showing the other ammeter readings.

c) What do these readings prove about the current in any circuit.

3 Below is a diagram of a polythene rod that has been rubbed with a cloth.

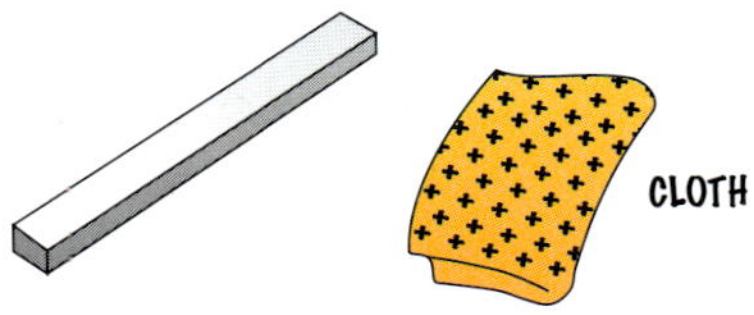

a) Copy the diagram and draw in the charge that the polythene rod would gain.

b) What has been 'scraped off' (and from which material) for the rod and the cloth to become charged up as above?

c) What happens when a perspex rod is rubbed with a cloth? Use diagrams to explain.

4 Below is a bar magnet. Copy and draw in its magnetic field.

a) Why is this a permanent magnetic field.

5 You are given a magnet whose poles are unknown. Explain using diagrams how you would determine the poles if all you have is another magnet whose poles are known.

6 Below is a simple electromagnet. Copy and draw in the magnetic field formed.

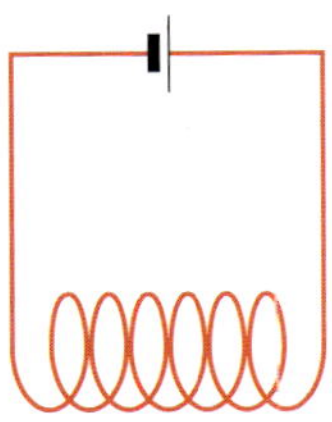

a) What is the difference between an electromagnet and an ordinary magnet?

b) Name 3 ways of increasing the strength of an electromagnet.

7 Below is a diagram of a relay which is a switch where a small current switches on a much larger current.

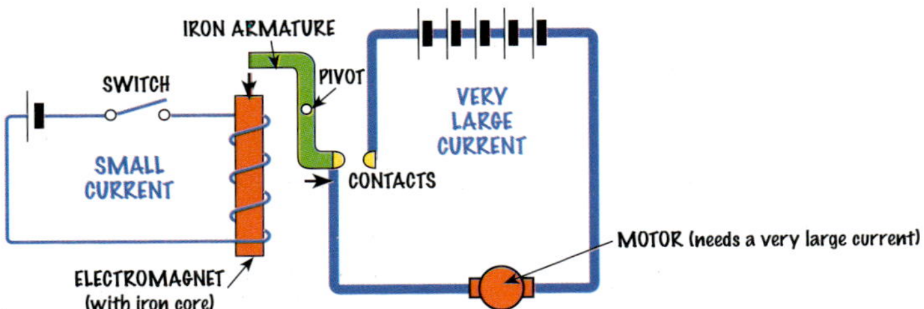

a) Explain how the relay works.

8 a) What is a force and what are they measured in? b) Below are 3 forces A, B and C in action? Name each force.

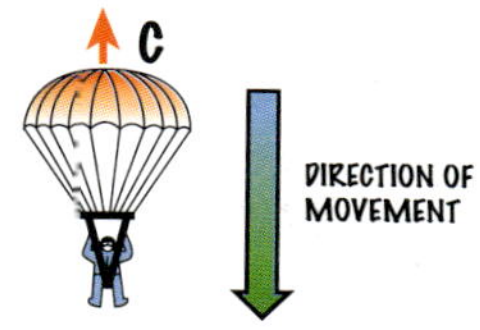

9 a) A car travels 120 kilometeres in 2 hours. What was the speed of the car?

b) If the car keeps travelling at that speed for another 40 minutes, how far will it travel?

c) If an athlete is capable of running at a constant speed of 5 metres per second, how long would the athlete take to run the distance the car travels in part b). Give your answer in both seconds and minutes.

10 a) A man weighing 1000N wears shoes of total area $400cm^2$. What pressure would he exert on the ground.

b) What would happen to the pressure he exerts if he stood on one foot only?

11 Give one practical example involving pressure where a) a large surface area is essential.

b) a small surface area is essential.

12 Opposite is a seesaw with two children on it.

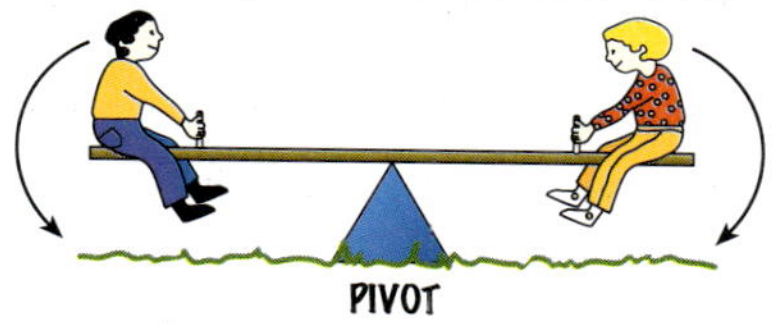

The boy weighs 600N and the girl 400N.

a) The boy sits 1.5m from the pivot. What moment does he exert? b) The girl sits on the pivot. What moment does she exert? c) Is the seesaw balanced?, if not explain what the girl has to do in order for the seesaw to become balanced.

13 Which form of energy, ...

a) is stored in an object which has been stretched or compressed?

b) does a moving motor car have?

c) is provided by a battery?

d) does water at the top of a waterfall have?

e) is created by any vibrating object?

14 A light bulb is supplied with 60 Joules of electrical energy. Explain why it does not give out 60 Joules of light energy.

15 a) Draw a diagram to show how a shadow is formed.

b) What are the two ways of increasing the size of the shadow. Draw diagrams to illustrate your answers.

16 A mirror has a ray of light incident on it where the angle between the ray and the mirror is 30° as shown below.

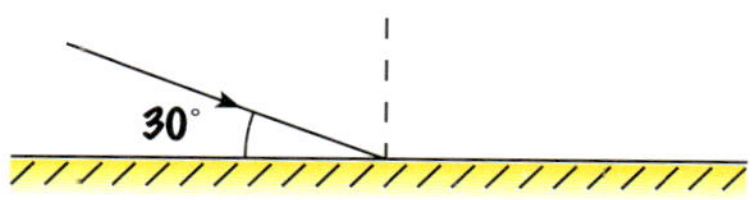

Copy and complete the diagram to show how the ray of light is reflected.

17 a) Copy and complete the following diagram.

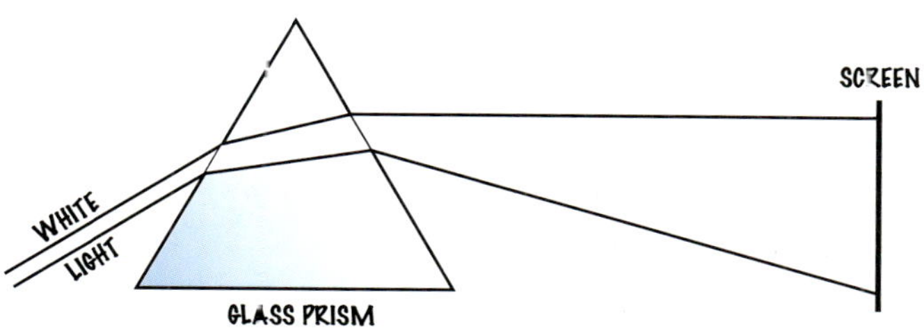

b) What is the effect called?

c) What are the different colours called?

d) A green filter is placed between the source of the white light and the glass prism. What effect would this have?

18 a) Draw a simple labelled diagram showing the orbits of the four inner most planets going around the sun.

b) Explain why the two planets nearer the sun take less time to orbit.

19 a) What is a Satellite? b) Name TWO natural satellites of the Sun? c) Name the natural satellite of the Earth?

d) What is an artificial satellite? e) Name THREE ways that artificial satellites are used.

INDEX

PROGRESS AND REVISION CHART

Page No.	Section No.	Section Title	Covered in Class	Revised	Revised
4	1	Life Processes			
5	2	Cells			
6	3	Constituents of Food			
7	4	Digesting Food			
8	5	Circulatory System			
9	6	The Lungs and Gas Exchange			
10	7	Respiration			
11	8	Bones, Joints and Muscles			
12	9	Adolescence and Reproduction			
13	10	Fertilisation and Development			
14	11	Health I			
15	12	Health II			
16	13	Photosynthesis			
17	14	Plant Reproduction I			
18	15	Plant Reproduction II			
19	16	Variation and Selective Breeding			
20	17	Classification of Living Things			
21	18	Using Keys to Identify Organisms			
22	19	Adaptation to Environment			
23	20	Food Webs and Food Chains			
24	21	Pyramids of Numbers			
25	22	Competition and Survival			

28	1	Materials and Their Properties I			
29	2	Materials and Their Properties II			
30	3	Solids, Liquids and Gases I			
31	4	Solids, Liquids and Gases II			
32	5	Expansion, Contraction and Change of State			
33	6	Diffusion and Gas Pressure			
34	7	Soils and Rocks			
35	8	The Rock Cycle			
36	9	Elements			
37	10	Compounds			
38	11	Mixtures			

PROGRESS AND REVISION CHART

Page No.	Section No.	Section Title	Covered in Class	Revised	Revised
39	12	Solutions - Another Type of Mixture			
40	13	Separating Mixtures I			
41	14	Separating Mixtures I I			
42	15	Physical and Chemical Change			
43	16	Chemical Reactions			
44	17	Oxidation Reactions			
45	18	Non Useful Oxidation Reactions			
46	19	The Reactions of Metals with Oxygen, Water & Acid			
47	20	Displacement Reactions			
48	21	Acids and Alkalis			
49	22	Reactions of Acids			
50	23	Chemistry Odds and Ends			

53	1	Static Electricity			
54	2	Simple Circuits			
55	3	Electric Current			
56	4	Magnetic Fields			
57	5	Electromagnets			
58	6	Forces			
59	7	Balanced and Unbalanced Forces			
60	8	Pressure			
61	9	Moments			
62	10	Speed			
63	11	Forms of Energy			
64	12	Energy Resources			
65	13	Transfer of Energy			
66	14	Light			
67	15	Reflection and Refraction of Light			
68	16	Colour			
69	17	Sound			
70	18	The Solar System			
71	19	The Sun, Earth and Moon			
72	20	Apparent Movement of The Sun and Stars			
73	21	Satellites			

NOTES

Arsenal are great ⓪va